Jeff Greenfield

TELEVISION
PRIME TIME·NEWS·SPORTS

Compliments of Home Savings of America

New York *Daily News* gossip columnist
Ed Sullivan hosted *Toast of the Town*
in 1948. Its first show starred, among
others, the new comedy team of Dean
Martin and Jerry Lewis. Although
Sullivan completely lacked any gift for
entertaining, his Sunday night show
brought a wide range of talent to
television. In 1964, Sullivan featured the
Beatles, probably the most popular rock
act of all time.

Editor: Lory Frankel
Designer: Nai Chang

Library of Congress Catalog Card Number: 80-68005
International Standard Book Number: 0-8109-2239-8
Originally published as part of a larger work titled
TELEVISION: THE FIRST FIFTY YEARS
© 1977, 1980 Harry N. Abrams, B.V.

VARIETY

The first promise of television was elemental: for the first time, in the comfort and privacy of their living rooms, people could see what was happening, as it was happening, right before their eyes. The sheer presence of pictures, of talent, of movement was enough in the early days of television to hypnotize an audience. And thus, the first major successes on television—apart from borrowed forms such as wrestling matches and old Hopalong Cassidy movies—were variety shows. In 1948, three of the most important early television shows made their debuts: *The Texaco Star Theatre*, with Milton Berle; *Arthur Godfrey's Talent Scouts*; and *Toast of the Town*, with Ed Sullivan. A year later, Sid Caesar and Imogene Coca came on the air with *The Admiral Broadway Revue*, later changed to *Your Show of Shows*.

Yet these four shows sharply diverged in their approach and format, creating a number of distinct patterns in variety shows that run through the development of the medium. In particular, the Berle and Sullivan shows relied heavily on excitement, on a sense of show business pace that is traceable to the days of vaudeville and the fast-moving, gala Broadway revues. Arthur Godfrey, in his personality and in the format of his shows, represented the relaxed, informal, "homey" approach, which used the television set less as a bridge into a glamorous world of show business and more as a harmonious part of the living room itself. This approach has subsequently flourished from daytime to late night.

Consider *The Texaco Star Theatre*. An orchestra plays an up-tempo tune as a quartet of gas-station attendants sing the opening theme. They introduce, to drumrolls, the star, Milton Berle. He appears suddenly, dressed in an outlandish costume—perhaps as the Easter Bunny or a giant valentine heart; often he was in women's clothing. He strides around the stage, mugging, leering, his face a rubber mask of contortions. He introduces the first act: jugglers, acrobats, or perhaps an animal act. Something for the eye; something you can see. The jokes are right out of burlesque: the seltzer squirt, the pie in the face, the cry of "Maaaakeup!" followed by a makeup puff right in Berle's face.

Consider the Sullivan show, the acts following one another in dizzy succession: jugglers, acrobats, dan-

The outrageous comedy of Milton Berle on *The Texaco Star Theatre* in 1948 was the first major success on commercial television. In this NBC Tuesday night show, Berle paraded across the stage in outlandish dress. He made himself the butt of the show's humor, with wisecracking assistants (such as Arnold Stang; *left*) who put down the king of comedy. Berle merged his talent with another early television success, *Howdy Doody (bottom;* Buffalo Bob Smith, center, and the childlike Clarabell, right, are shown here along with Berle as cutup kid). Comedian Martha Raye and singer-dancer Ray Bolger *(below, left)* join Berle in one of the later shows before the Berle phenomenon burned itself out.

Your Show of Shows began on NBC in 1950 on Saturday nights. Although it presented a variety of singers, dancers, and comedians, the show's centerpiece was the comedy team of Sid Caesar and Imogene Coca *(top)*. They were backed by the talents of second banana Carl Reiner *(above; right)* and Howard Morris, and a writing stable with some of the funniest television writers the medium ever employed, including Mel Brooks, Neil Simon, and Larry Gelbart.

cers, animal acts ("I was booked on the Sullivan show," Don Rickles once cracked, "but my bear died"). His show featured masses of people: the West Point Glee Club, the New York City Ballet. He turned live cameras on a fireworks display in the New York City harbor ("Let's really hear it for the fireworks!" he implored his audience).

Even the Caesar show, remembered for the brilliant comic talents of Caesar, Coca, Carl Reiner, and Howard Morris, and a writing team that included Neil Simon and Mel Brooks, featured the Billy Williams Quartet, Marguerite Piazza, the Bob Hamilton Trio, and dancers Bambi Linn and Rod Alexander, both to break the pace of the skits and to provide visual entertainment.

Arthur Godfrey was a different kind of performer. His appeal, both on the *Talent Scouts* show and on *Arthur Godfrey and His Friends*, depended less on excitement and more on the public warmth and accessibility of Godfrey himself. His show was an offering of familial affection. Announcer Tony Marvin, singers Frank Parker and Marion Marlowe (were they really in love?), the McGuire Sisters, Haleloke, singer Julius LaRosa, and bandleader Archie Bleyer were not just professionals. Godfrey talked to them, let the viewers know them as people. The reality of conflict, the on-the-air firing of LaRosa, did not matter. For Godfrey had provided a method of reaching the television audience that was particularly well-suited to the medium. He had an instinctive understanding that this living-room furniture, intimately present in the homes of viewers, could be made an enormously powerful substitute for real familial bonds.

These first variety shows, then, displayed three distinct forms: first, the host as talent (Caesar and Berle), blending his or her skills into a broadly appealing show. Second, the host as broker of talent (Sullivan), offering a blend of comedy, song, dance, and spectacle. Third, the host as friend (Godfrey), subordinating talent to the fact of his presence. What is curious—and revealing—is that the medium tended to provide far more longevity to the last two categories than to the first.

Milton Berle, the first giant star of television, the man who closed down restaurants and movie theaters at eight o'clock on Tuesday nights, was soundly beaten in the ratings by Phil Silvers's army situation comedy, *You'll Never Get Rich*, and taken off the air in 1956, long since deposed as ratings king. Sid Caesar was conquered by Lawrence Welk in 1957, but he had lost his Saturday night spot by 1954. These outsized talents were burned out by television; it was almost as if they could not survive the expending of so much sheer energy. By contrast, Ed Sullivan remained on the air for twenty-three years.

This is not to say that talent does not survive on television in the variety format. Red Skelton lasted on CBS

A low-key, low-pressure, informal radio star named Arthur Godfrey made an easy transition to television in the late 1940s. For years he had two weekly prime-time shows, *Arthur Godfrey's Talent Scouts,* and *Arthur Godfrey and His Friends* (Godfrey is shown here, with Dr. Frank Stanton, then president of CBS, center, and Hawaiian singer Haleloke, far right). Note the studied informality of the set, as if he and his friends were having an evening of fun in his living room.

Red Skelton, shown here as Freddie the Freeloader, one of his enduring characters, was a mainstay of the CBS prime-time schedule for more than a decade.

Jack Benny (shown here with Irish tenor Dennis Day) so carefully cultivated his image on radio that the transition to television was easy. His variety show was actually a situation comedy about a stingy comedian named Jack Benny, and the misadventures he and his colleagues had in putting on a television show.

for nearly twenty years; Jack Benny had a run on CBS television that lasted fifteen years; Carol Burnett has been on CBS for a decade; and Bob Hope was an NBC drawing card for more than twenty years. Talent, however, is not enough. Television seems to demand from its variety principals a particular kind of personality: low-key, easygoing, friendly, amiable. A warm personality can survive without talent. So can a personality audiences come to know and trust, even without the warmth; Ed Sullivan is a prime example. Talent without that personality cannot succeed.

Some of radio's most popular personalities could not make the transition successfully into television. The zany Ed Wynn, the acerbic Fred Allen were two early examples. Singers who were enormously gifted, compelling in person and on records, tried and failed at regular television variety shows—Frank Sinatra and Judy Garland are two prime examples. Those that made the transition had something more to commend them to television audiences. Among radio personalities, Jack Benny had built such a strong *per-*

Two of the long-distance runners of television, Jack Benny and Bob Hope, here join forces. CBS's "capture" of Benny from NBC in the late 1940s gave that network its first success against NBC as a prime-time ratings champion. Hope has been a mainstay of NBC—with both regular shows and specials—since the earliest days of television.

One of the most successful variety shows of the late 1950s starred Garry Moore (*top*; left), an amiable performer of no particular talent. His announcer, sidekick, and commercial spokesman, Durwood Kirby, was of similar dimensions. But a female second banana, Carol Burnett, went on to host what is now the longest running and most successful prime-time variety show on the air. She's shown (*above*) with long-time regular, Harvey Korman.

Judy Garland, shown here in 1956 on a *General Electric Theatre* special, was one of many supremely talented performers who could not sustain a weekly television show.

"Lonesome George Gobel" was a Saturday night star in the late 1950s, popularizing homey expressions ("Well, I'll be a dirty bird"). Along with many variety hosts, Gobel built a situation-comedy sketch into the variety format.

Fred Allen was one of the giants of radio comedy, with an acerbic wit and a deliberate posture of "anti-friendliness." He did not, however, do well on television; after this 1953 attempt, he was generally confined to panel shows.

sona, such a family of supporting characters, that he was in fact part of a situation comedy in the guise of a variety show. (Many long-running variety shows presented situation comedies as part of the variety show, most notably Jackie Gleason with "The Honeymooners," which later became a half-hour comedy. Carol Burnett today has one of the most brutally funny "mini-sit-coms," with her "Family.") Among singers who made the switch, Dinah Shore and Perry Como, both with easygoing charm, have survived for years as successful television performers.

As television moved west, as the filmed series became the dominant TV mode, as syndication of film became the surest route to big money, the appeal of the live variety show faded for producers. With their use of topical jokes and contemporary songs and guest stars, they proved impossible to syndicate for reruns once their network runs were over. This meant that the biggest source of windfall profits was fore-

Dinah Shore, who succeeded in both prime time and daytime, combined singing talent, a "perky" personality, and a big goodnight kiss to win her audiences. Louis Prima and Keely Smith, George Montgomery and Dinah, Ernie Kovacs and Edie Adams—all married couples at the time—came together here.

Jackie Gleason as Ralph Kramden, bus driver, and Art Carney as Ed Norton, sewer worker, share a moment of intellectual curiosity in Kramden's apartment in *The Honeymooners*. In reruns today, *The Honeymooners* still comes across as one of the funniest situation comedies.

His relaxed mood sparked many jokes ("Did you see Perry Como?" "No, I fell asleep." "So did he."), but Perry Como starred in a high-rated NBC variety show. He still draws audiences to his specials.

Despite their amiable manner, the Smothers Brothers, in the late 1960s, starred in one of the few hit variety shows to stand in direct opposition to mainstream values. Tom and Dick are shown here with two well-known television couples, Barbara Bain and Martin Landau (then from *Mission: Impossible*), and Sonny and Cher.

One of the more inventive variety shows in its use of television was Flip Wilson's NBC Thursday night show of the early 1970s.

Rowan and Martin's Laugh-In borrowed liberally from such diverse sources as burlesque, vaudeville, and early television creators like Steve Allen and Ernie Kovacs. The fast-paced, often freewheeling one-hour show was aimed at an audience used to the quick cuts and instant transitions of television. Everyone from John Wayne to Richard Nixon cooperated in filming cameo shots. *Laugh-In* also provided the first showcase for Tiny Tim (center) and "Tiptoe Through the Tulips."

closed to variety performers and producers. At the same time, as television became a familiar presence in the American living room, the original premise of the variety format became untenable; it was no longer enough simply to show the viewers that something was happening in front of their eyes. Those variety shows that succeeded in prime time had to offer something special. In the late 1960s, the Smothers Brothers beat the once invincible western, *Bonanza*, by being the first explicitly antiwar, antiestablishment television show. In their comedy skits, in their choice of guests (Pete Seeger, Joan Baez), in their public battles with the CBS network, the Smothers Brothers were unique: an act with mass public appeal that was in opposition to mainstream values. Their public disputes proved too much for the network, which canceled the show in the spring of 1969.

Flip Wilson achieved success as a variety show host—the first black to do so—with a format that was clearly adjusted to the world of television. Most variety shows worked off a proscenium stage, with the televi-

sion camera in effect occupying "the best seat in the house." Wilson's show was mounted as theater-in-the-round, with the audience surrounding the stage, and used light, mobile sets and a minimum of props. In this sense, the show acknowledged Bertolt Brecht's principle of alienation; the audience was always aware that it was watching a television show. As the skits ended, the camera would pull back to show the movement of sets and actors.

Probably no show used the medium of television more aggressively than *Rowan and Martin's Laugh-In* on NBC. From the time it began in January, 1968, it captivated the audience, especially the younger viewers who had grown up with television. While the show's popularity was relatively short-lived—it was canceled in 1973—the use of black-outs, fast-paced cutting, and constant flash-backs and flash-forwards was innovative. Although it owed a debt to television's original mad genius, Ernie Kovacs, it was much more experimental than the conventional variety show. *Laugh-In* was also politically and sexually open; hosts Dan

From 1950 in Philadelphia, through four television networks, until his death in 1962 while creating monthly specials for ABC—no one was more creative, no one pushed the comic possibilities of television further than did Ernie Kovacs. He created a raft of characters (Bavarian Disk Jockey Wolfgang Sauerbraten is one of them), parodied old television shows, and played visual tricks on his audiences through such devices as chromakeying (rendering people and objects invisible) and mixing images.

Late-night television began in earnest with NBC's *Broadway Open House (above),* featuring the antics of knockabout comic Jerry Lester. He is shown here with accordionist Milton de Lugg and Dagmar, whose appeal Lester exploited ceaselessly. Steve Allen *(above, right)* later took over the show (renamed *The Tonight Show),* and presided over a low-key, informal collection of singers (Steve Lawrence and Eydie Gormé), comics, and offbeat personalities such as Ben Belafont, the rhyming inventor. Watching Jack Paar *(right;* center, flanked by singer Geneviève and Cliff Arquette as Charlie Weaver), who hosted *The Tonight Show* from 1957 until 1962, was like watching a tipsy aerialist working without a net. He was nervous, contentious, self-obsessed—and it often led to compelling television. Paar walked off his show once in 1960 to protest censorship.

Rowan and Dick Martin gibed at politicians without irritating the network the way the Smothers Brothers alienated the executives at CBS. (Despite the liberal tone of the show, the politician who benefited most from *Laugh-In* was Richard Nixon, who as the 1968 Republican presidential nominee appeared in a black-out sequence asking "Sock it to *me*?" in an attempt to prove he was able to laugh at himself.)

While the variety format was struggling to regain a place in prime time—at one point in 1975 there were only two prime-time variety shows on the three networks combined—it became securely ensconced all across the rest of the television day by applying the fundamental premise that Godfrey had brought to television—the premise of informality.

The Tonight Show, which first began as Jerry Lester's *Broadway Open House,* was launched in 1954 as a part of NBC president Sylvester "Pat" Weaver's notion of a magazine-format show to occupy early morning, midday, and late-night television. (He succeeded at all but the midday idea, where Arlene Francis's *Home* lasted four seasons.) Under a succession of hosts, from Steve Allen to Jack Paar to Johnny Carson (with a disastrous interlude when Jack Lescoulie was

For fifteen years, late-night television in America has meant *The Tonight Show* with Johnny Carson, a comedian with a naughty-boy quality and a capacity to reinforce the audience's expectations with almost ritualistic repetition. An unusual event was the wedding of Tiny Tim and "Miss Vicky," held on a show of December, 1969 *(below)*. On a quieter night, Carson chats with then–New York Mayor John Lindsay, Bill Cosby, and announcer Ed McMahon *(left)*.

host), the show became progressively more formal, in the sense that there were locked-in nightly rituals. Allen was always good for a fling into the audience or a spontaneous burst of offbeat humor. Jack Paar was sufficiently moody to launch a feud, as he did with columnists Walter Winchell and Dorothy Kilgallen. But Johnny Carson has succeeded for fifteen years not just because of a superb sense of comic timing, but by providing his late-night audience with a comfortable, reassuring presence. They know he will mock his monologue; they know that his sidekick, Ed McMahon, will laugh excessively; they know Carson will make fun of Doc Severinsen's wardrobe, McMahon's drinking, Burbank's senior citizens.

The look, the set, the feel of *The Tonight Show* and of syndicated talk-variety shows with such popular hosts as Merv Griffin, Mike Douglas, and Dinah Shore negate the original premise of "show business." They do not glitter; they are not glamorous; they are not even very exciting. They are designed to make the audience feel that the show is a part of their neighborhood, part of their home environment, where interesting people come and talk about the daily events of their lives: flying up to Vegas, working on a film, a humorous

The success of Carson has inspired many similar shows, with varying degrees of success. *The Merv Griffin Show (top)* worked well in syndication but failed as a CBS alternative to Carson (Griffin used Arthur Treacher as his Ed McMahon). Mike Douglas *(center)* has been on the air for more than fifteen years (he's shown here with Ella Fitzgerald, Fred Astaire, and Gene Kelly). Dick Cavett *(above)* offered a more thoughtful mix of talk than did Carson—he's shown here with Norman Mailer—but the late-night audience preferred Carson's polish.

adventure on vacation. These shows act, in fact, as surrogate salons, providing a sense of communal exchange to people who live increasingly atomized lives. The talk ought not be *too* pretentious or serious, as Dick Cavett learned. But these shows have succeeded because they have not sought to follow the old-fashioned Broadway show business tradition of "knocking the audiences out." Most television audiences don't *want* to be "knocked out." They want, instead, to be included in.

In recent years, an alternate current has begun to stir in variety programming. Some shows have sought to recapture the excitement and glamour of television's early days by exploiting the medium's visual appeal in a contemporary way—the color, the glitter, the lights, the costumes. The original *Sonny and Cher Comedy Hour*, which began in 1971, was the first effort in this direction. Cher's costumes were spectacular. The cameras caught the action from unique angles, often shooting directly out at the audience from behind the performers, capturing not only the cheering audience but the glint of spotlights. The acts were broken up by short bursts of animated tomfoolery—a debt to *Laugh-In*. The orchestrations were brassy and full.

The premise was that audiences could be awakened by the show business values that most variety shows, and in particular the informal, talk-show brand of variety show, had dispensed with. This premise was probably illustrated most spectacularly in the special that Cher Bono did as a solo show in 1975. Featuring Bette Midler, Elton John, and Flip Wilson, the special was an incredibly lavish display of satin, glitter, wild sets, and surrealistic effects.

The same principle was applied to the ABC variety show *Donny & Marie*, which began in January, 1976. The two principals, members of the highly successful Osmond family, are in one sense pure carbon copies of Sonny and Cher (although it must be a source of comfort to ABC executives that they cannot get divorced). They bicker with each other, insult one another, and have virtually no comic talent whatsoever. They are, however, enveloped in special effects. They are costumed in full color; the show begins each week with an ice-skating number. One regular feature of the show finds Donny and Marie singing with two different groups of back-up singers and two different orchestras.

This suggests that the variety format has come full circle. From a fascination with the purely visual attraction of television, the medium found that it could guarantee success most easily with a personality and a format that did not overwhelm the audience but blended in with it. More recently, an attempt has begun to wake the audience up; to remind it with color, sets, and costumes that television can still catch the eye of an increasingly jaded viewing audience.

An eighteen-year-old boy and a sixteen-year-old girl hosting their own television show? *Donny & Marie*, of the slickly polished Osmond family, debuted in 1976, surrounded by costumes, elaborate sets, and an ice follies feature.

The Brady Bunch, a situation comedy series from 1969 to 1974, was resuscitated by ABC as a variety special. It, too, relied heavily on elaborate visual props.

Studs Terkel came from Chicago. He was blacklisted from television because of his political views, but later gained renown as the author of *Working* and *Hard Times*. Here he hosts an early show, *Studs' Place*.

Many pioneers of "low-pressure" television variety came out of Chicago. Dave Garroway was the first to move in a direction alien to the New York-Broadway-nightclub style. Apart from his *Today* show work, he was host of *Garroway at Large*, originating from this crowded Chicago studio (shown in 1951).

Indiana-born Herb Shriner, a rural anecdotalist, turned that image into a television career, hosting quiz and variety shows. He's shown here on *The Herb Shriner Show* with an unlikely companion, Orson Welles.

Bishop Fulton J. Sheen was television's first religious "star"; his show, *Life Is Worth Living,* ran on ABC, where he appeared opposite Milton Berle.

A precursor of the celebrity talk show, enabling viewers to feel a sense of intimacy with the famous, was *The Stork Club,* ostensibly originating from Sherman Billingsley's famous New York night spot. In this 1950 show, Billingsley (right) talks with Kay Thompson, Ethel Merman, and an unidentified man.

He couldn't sing, dance, or tell a joke, but Art Linkletter had an affable way about him which audiences liked. He hosted game shows *(People Are Funny),* as well as a series of daytime variety shows, most notably *Art Linkletter's House Party* on CBS. This is a shot from *The Art Linkletter Show,* which ran on NBC in 1963.

NBC executive Sylvester "Pat" Weaver's midafternoon magazine-format show, *Home,* with Arlene Francis, lasted only a few years.

From 1969 to 1972, British personality David Frost hosted a syndicated nightly show, which pioneered the idea of interviewing a single guest—here, Shirley MacLaine. In 1977, Frost won headlines by interviewing—and paying $600,000 for the privilege—former president Richard Nixon.

Faye Emerson had her own show in the first days of television. Her décolletage once caused a national uproar. She poses here with the musical headliner of her show, Skitch Henderson.

A cross between a variety show, a game show, and ▶
an amateur talent show, *You Bet Your Life* featured the
comic abilities of Groucho Marx. Announcer George
Fenneman was his unflappable straight man.

One of the charms of *The Arthur Murray Party*
can be seen here: the mix of Kathryn Murray's
ebullience with Arthur's stony countenance.

To present the Broadway play *High Button Shoes*,
starring Phil Silvers, on television in 1948, cameras
were simply placed in front of the stage.

Sing Along with Mitch was a popular NBC show in the
early 1960s. The girl just under Miller's left arm is Leslie
Uggams, later a star of *Roots*.

NBC was the first to use a black performer
as host of a variety show, *The Nat King Cole
Show*, in 1956. Many Southern affiliates refused
to carry it, and it failed.

Singer Andy Williams *(left)* hosted a variety show in the tradition of Perry Como on NBC for several years in the 1960s and early 1970s. The Osmond Brothers *(above)* were regular performers on the show. The youngest one, Donny, on the far right, became cohost of *Donny & Marie* on ABC in 1976.

One of the first variety shows on television, starring one of the greats, Jimmy Durante, was *The All-Star Revue*, on NBC. Durante's partner, Eddie Jackson ("Of Clayton, Jackson, and Du-rante!"), is seen here.

A direct descendant of *Major Bowes and His Original Amateur Hour, Ted Mack and the Original Amateur Hour* stayed on the air for twenty-two years, featuring tap dancers, accordion players, and other greats from America's heartland.

Hee Haw featured country and Western music in a down-home setting. Despite high ratings, it was canceled because it drew primarily older or rural viewers.

In June, 1953, the Ford Motor Company celebrated its fiftieth anniversary with a show telecast on both CBS and NBC. The lavish special was and is best remembered for the pairing of two of Broadway's biggest musical stars, Mary Martin and Ethel Merman. They demonstrated that none of the special visual effects of TV could match pure talent as a means of creating viewer excitement.

Two extraordinary singing talents join forces on a 1967 *Kraft Music Hall* presentation: Liza Minnelli and the late Bobby Darin.

Satire is what closes on Saturday night—so goes an old Broadway adage. An attempt to import a British satirical show, *That Was the Week That Was (bottom, left),* failed in the mid-1960s. Later, public television brought over the madness of *Monty Python's Flying Circus (above)* to an enthusiastic audience. Here, playing the Dinsdale Brothers, are (from left) John Cleese, Michael Palin, Graham Chapman, Eric Idle, and Terry Jones. In 1975, NBC gave over the late-night Saturday slot to *Saturday Night,* an irreverent, frequently outrageous satirical show. Chevy Chase gained fame as an impersonator of President Ford. The *Saturday Night* regulars *(left)* are (from left) Danny Aykroyd, Jane Curtin, Garrett Morris, Laraine Newman, Gilda Radner, Bill Murray, and John Belushi (who also appears below).

◄ His politics are strictly conservative Republican, and he turned his military tours into political statements, but Bob Hope was still a widely popular figure, in large measure due to his frequent tours of American military bases abroad. He's shown here in a 1967 Christmas visit to Vietnam.

In addition to starring in a successful variety show, Carol Burnett teamed up with other performers to create memorable specials. Julie Andrews was one of her favorite companions.

This 1967 special, "Sinatra: A Man and His Music," shows what television can do when it stays away from cloying cuteness and lets two great performers perform. Just Sinatra, Ella Fitzgerald, and songs.

The Academy Awards, symbol of the movie industry which once regarded television with such fear, has become an annual production spectacular, and one of the most popular shows of the year. Bob Hope hosts the twenty-fifth anniversary of the awards in 1953 *(below)*. For all the lavishly spent dollars, however, one of the charms of the Academy Awards is that it is live; there is always the possibility of the unexpected. In 1973, Sacheen Littlefeather *(right)* accepted Marlon Brando's Academy Award with a speech on Indian rights.

One of the traditions established by television was the musical version of *Peter Pan* with Mary Martin, presented by NBC in 1955, and shown for years after. The same network broadcast *Amahl and the Night Visitors (below)* in 1951, the first opera commissioned for television, written by Gian-Carlo Menotti. It was for fifteen years a traditional Christmastime presentation.

The NBC Symphony Orchestra, an example of radio's partnership with serious music, was founded in 1937 under the baton of Arturo Toscanini. It survived into the television era, but after Toscanini's retirement in 1954 it was disbanded. And serious music all but disappeared from commercial television.

SITUATION COMEDY

More than any other form, the situation comedy is the bedrock of regular American television. Variety shows have flourished and faded; dramatic shows have gone from live anthology presentations to filmed series, from cops to cowboys to doctors and back to cops; singers and bandleaders have long since been discarded by television programmers as prime-time stars. But the situation comedy has endured throughout television history—indeed, throughout broadcasting history—with the essential form all but untouched. The content has changed in the days from *I Love Lucy* to *The Mary Tyler Moore Show*, the subject matter has been broadened from *Fibber McGee and Molly* to *All in the Family* and *Maude,* but situation comedy has become the most predictable of prime-time offerings. And predictability is precisely the reason for situation-comedy success. For these shows, virtually without exception, embody the central premise of American television programming: they give us characters whose habits, foibles, and responses to situations we know as we know those of our own friends and family. What's more, these characters—unlike real people—do not deviate from their habits. They provide a sense of family warmth without confusion, without ambiguity.

From the first days of network radio, situation comedy touched a nerve in the audience. In March of 1928, the National Broadcasting Company began broadcasting *Amos 'n' Andy*, a fifteen-minute show created and acted by Freeman Fisher Gosden and Charles J. Correll. The show dealt with the comic adventures of a pair of South Side Chicago Negroes who ran the Fresh Air Taxi Cab Company of America, "Incorpulated," and whose social life revolved around the Mystic Knights of the Sea lodge, presided over by the Kingfish.

Most current observers who look back on *Amos 'n' Andy* see it as a mean-spirited exploitation of racial stereotypes. And, indeed, the mocking approach to black upward mobility, the mangling of the English language ("I'se re-*gusted*," "Splain dat to me"), and the fact that two white men played the Negro characters were all strong elements of racism. (The show was moved to television in 1951, with a black cast—Tim Moore as the Kingfish displayed a brilliant comedic hand—but the growing anger over black stereotyping drove the show off the air and ultimately out of syndication by 1966.) More significant is the fact that this first broadcasting sit-com hit contained many of the ingre-

Two miscreants in search of adventure, wealth, or just some peace and quiet: it was the premise of the first broadcast situation comedy, *Amos 'n' Andy,* a huge radio success and long a hardy perennial. Freeman Gosden and Charles Correll, both white, played the two on radio.

Amos 'n' Andy's formula of pairing two trouble-prone males was often employed. Jackie Gleason and Art Carney in *The Honeymooners (right)* worked their mischief under the suspicious gaze of Audrey Meadows as Alice Kramden. Abbott and Costello *(far right)* were paired on NBC in the early days of television, and they are still seen in reruns. A more contemporary example *(farthest right)* is the television version of Neil Simon's hit play, *The Odd Couple,* with Tony Randall *(right)* and Jack Klugman. (Later the ladies got into the act, as in *Laverne & Shirley.*)

dients that remain a part of the form almost fifty years later.

The characters are in a situation which is in essence unchanging. The taxicab company will *always* be a laughably small enterprise, with a tiny office and a single chair. The grand dreams of Amos will always be laughably impossible to realize. Kingfish will always be the operator, looking for the quick deal, and Andy will always be his victim. The supporting characters—the awesomely stupid Lightnin', the pompous Lawyer Calhoun—will be exactly the same, day in and day out. Even the vocabulary, the phrases used by the characters, will remain unvarying.

These elements remain intact no matter which situation comedy is examined. Many of them—*The Honeymooners*, with Jackie Gleason, Art Carney, and Audrey Meadows, to take a famous example—feature characters in economic straits who have dreams of success. A look at the apartment of Ralph and Alice Kramden reveals almost-desperate poverty: an ancient icebox, an old sink, a table with four chairs and always the same checked tablecloth, a bureau. Kramden is not content with his sorry lot: he is going to become a

supervisor; he is going to get rich quick with a kitchen appliance; he is going to impress a wealthy acquaintance by socializing with him on the golf course.

The set-up—and the viewers' prior knowledge of the habits of these characters—establishes the humor. They know that Ed Norton will advise Kramden with a wild assortment of misinformation. They know that whenever Norton must write something, he will prepare for the task with an elaborate series of hand gestures, which will provoke Kramden to fury (*"Will you cut that out, Norton!?!"*). They know that Alice will be the voice of resigned reason, urging Ralph to reconsider his current scheme, and that they will clash (*"One of these days . . . one of these days, Alice—pow, right in the kisser!"*). They know that the plan will collapse as Kramden suffers the tortures of the damned (*" . . . hamma, hamma, hamma . . ."*), and that he will be consoled in the arms of his endlessly forgiving Alice (*"Baby, you're the greatest!"*).

The utter predictability of what a character will do, given his habits, quirks, and foibles, far from boring the listening or viewing audience enriches the humor, because it brings to any one joke or dilemma a knowledge

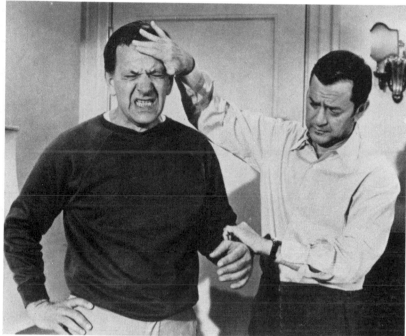

of that character's response. One of the funniest single moments in broadcasting, which took place on Jack Benny's radio show, provides a classic example of an audience completing the joke through its expectations. Benny, who had long established himself as one of the world's stingiest human beings, is on his way home late at night when he is accosted by a holdup man.

"Your money or your life!" the robber demands.

And then there is silence. Long, long moments of silence. Well before the irrelevant punchline ("I'm *thinking, I'm thinking!*"), the audience dissolved in laughter, fully grasping the predicament of the lovable tightwad. Similarly, in the long-running radio show *Fibber McGee and Molly*, Fibber's casual line about looking for a missing object in his closet triggered a wave of laughter. The audience knew that the famous, overcrowded closet would dislodge a mountain of junk on Fibber's head as soon as he opened the door. It did not need the inevitable payoff, the cascade of debris, to trigger the laugh. The joke arises from the situation itself, from a clearly defined character confronting a problem—as writer-producer Carl Reiner put it, "the interplay of situation and character." That is why, he said, "if someone asked

me what was the best comedy line I have ever written, I would have to say it was probably a line like 'I see,' or 'Ah-hah!' "

The requirement of situation comedy, then, is a set of characters that the audience will laugh at—and with—and care about. It's the *character* that's the key. Some of the most famous and well-liked entertainment figures of their time have failed to make a success out of situation comedies, because the audience could not be persuaded to care about them in the show's frame of reference. Stars such as Ray Bolger, Jack Lemmon, Bing Crosby, Ed Wynn, Ronald Colman, Gertrude Berg (in *Mrs. G Goes to College*, not *The Goldbergs*), Mickey Rooney, Pat O'Brien, Ezio Pinza, James Stewart, and Doris Day have been unable to transfer their popularity to the characters they were portraying.

Conversely, Lucille Ball, television's first situation-comedy superstar, managed to convince her television audience that she was the scatterbrained, childlike, troublemaking wife of a Cuban bandleader in *I Love Lucy*. As a movie actress, Lucille Ball frequently played glamorous, sophisticated women. The television audience, however, accepted her as a broad comic figure.

The all-time comedy queen of television was Lucille Ball. Beginning in 1951, she was a weekly performer on CBS for twenty-three years. Older television viewers remember her best in *I Love Lucy*, with Desi Arnaz as bandleader Ricky Ricardo, and Vivian Vance and William Frawley as neighbors Fred and Ethel Mertz. The show relied on a heavy dose of slapstick, at which Lucille Ball proved herself without peer. Of course it was unbelievable—but it was very funny.

It accepted her so thoroughly that in 1977, twenty-six years after *I Love Lucy* began on CBS, films of the original shows with Ball, Desi Arnaz, and Vivian Vance and William Frawley as the neighborly Fred and Ethel Mertz, are still running on local stations all over America.

So the question is, how do successful situation comedies win over audiences? How do they make us not simply laugh at comic antics, but care about the principal characters? To a remarkably uniform extent, the key device is the creation of a *family*—either in a home situation, a work situation, or both—that bonds each character to the other, and, in turn, bonds the audience to the characters. The familial bond in situation comedy exists for the same reason that so many characters in dramatic series live alone. The goal in dramatic series is to forge a bond between audience and character that rises out of concern, fear, jeopardy. The viewers are his only companions in his battle against evil or disease or danger. In situation comedy, loneliness is anathema. Not only is there no one to "play off," no ready source of comic conflict, there is also no fundamental sense of security that underlies the dilemma in which a comic figure finds himself or herself. There must be someone—family or friends who act as family—to ease the troubles of a comic figure with a comforting word or sense of concern.

The familial bond in situation comedy is all but total. Television comedy that has tried to make people laugh without the "safety net" of continuing, sympathetic characters has as a rule failed to attract a sufficient audience to enable it to survive, no matter how brilliant. Ernie Kovacs, the mad video genius of the 1950s and early 1960s who made the technology of television work as his humorous frame of reference, earned the distinc-

tion of having shows canceled by four television networks—CBS, ABC, NBC, and the now-defunct Du Mont television network. His inventiveness is legendary: musical pieces "played" by household appliances and foods; people vanishing in midair, or suddenly "shrunk" against giant pencils; tilted sets "straightened" by camerawork, so that olives rolled off "even" tables and milk poured crazily out of a thermos bottle. But the comedy of Kovacs could no more be contained in a series format than it could be explained by still photographs. It was comedy beyond the boundaries of a series, or even of a variety show with conventional skits. And it never found a mass audience.

More important, it is impossible to list a single situation comedy where a single lead character confronted the world; it simply is not the way the genre works. The familial bond forms an unbroken chain from the earliest days of radio, through *Life of Riley* and *The Dick Van Dyke Show*, to the most "daring" comedies of Norman Lear. Whatever the controversial nature of the topics treated in contemporary comedies—abortion, impotence, menopause, homosexuality—no producer has as yet dared to break with the form of a close-knit, family-style relationship. At times, in fact, comedies make deliberate adjustments in order to create a closer relationship between characters.

In its first year and a half, for example, the ABC comedy *Happy Days* was a "marginal" show; its ratings, while adequate, did not insure its survival. The core of this recollection of teenage life in the 1950s was the Cunningham family, an agonizingly normal archeological dig: pudgy, hapless father; wise, everything-will-be-all-right mother; an overachieving Henry Aldrich of a teenage son; and a kid sister. The spice in the stew was

No pretense of "reality" with vaudevillians George Burns and Gracie Allen in *The George Burns and Gracie Allen Show;* Burns would often interrupt the "plot" to make a few observations, punctuated by the ever-present cigar. Harry Von Zell, the show's announcer (left), was also the comic foil.

Women in early television were locked into traditional roles, but they weren't always docile. Eve Arden, in *Our Miss Brooks (top, left),* portrayed a sharp-tongued schoolteacher who drove the principal, played by Gale Gordon, to distraction. Ann Sothern played Don Porter's acerbic *Private Secretary (above;* on the right is Joel Grey).

These are two different situation-comedy families. William Bendix, who inherited the title role from Jackie Gleason in *Life of Riley (top, right),* was a paradigm dumb father, given to moaning "What a revoltin' development *this* is" at every crisis. His family included (from right) Marjorie Reynolds, Lugene Sanders, and Wesley Morgan. More than a decade later, *The Dick Van Dyke Show (bottom, right)* starred Van Dyke (far left) as a successful comedy writer, married to Mary Tyler Moore (far right). Morey Amsterdam and Rose Marie, his writer-colleagues and friends, provided the broader comic relief.

Two escapist views of youth: *Dobie Gillis (below)* was adapted from Max Shulman's stories of campus life in the late 1930s, updated to the late 1950s. Dwayne Hickman (second from left) played Dobie, with Bob Denver as his beatnik friend Maynard (far left), Sheila James as a girl nursing an unrequited love for Dobie, and Stephen Franken as rich snob Chatsworth Osborne, Jr. In 1975, ABC launched *Welcome Back, Kotter (right)*. Gabriel Kaplan plays the teacher who presides over the lovable antics of Barbarino (John Travolta), Washington (Lawrence Hilton-Jacobs), Epstein (Robert Hegyes), and Horshack (Ron Palillo). Marcia Strassman plays Kotter's wife, and John Sylvester White portrays Mr. Woodman.

the motorcycle-driving Arthur Fonzarelli, a super-cool defanged Wild One who knew the deepest mysteries of women and the art of being Cool. The problem was that Fonzarelli—"The Fonz"—was an outsider with no family bond and no ties to anyone else in the show except when he assumed the role of teacher to the unsophisticated teenagers.

So, in the fall of 1975, *Happy Days* creator Garry Marshall changed the show by having The Fonz rent out the attic apartment above the Cunninghams' garage, thus making him a surrogate member of the family.

"I knew," Marshall recalled after the show had become the number-one regular series in the ratings, "that if I got him over the garage, I could get him into the kitchen; he could 'become' a member of the family."

The first show of that season featured The Fonz losing his cool and approaching tears as he explained to the Cunninghams that he'd never known a real family before. That confession convinced the reluctant father to rent Fonzie the room, and helped to humanize the character, tempering his "cool" with vulnerability. It was also the beginning of the shift of Henry Winkler's "Fonzie" from a fairly popular supporting character in a

marginal television show to a national folk hero in the most popular show in America.

If there is one consistently dishonest element in every situation comedy, no matter how realistic, how bold, how relevant or controversial it may be, it is that no one in a situation comedy is isolated, alone, atomized. In a country where family bonds are dissolving, where broken marriages are increasing almost geometrically, and where the trend of living alone is becoming an important national fact of life, the world of the situation comedy depicts strong bonds between friends, coworkers, and family. No one sits home at night watching television; the most pervasive habit in American life today usually goes unrecorded in even the most "realistic" comedies because it is not funny. Instead, the sturdiest barriers of isolation vanish under the power of the family bond. The students of Gabe Kotter in *Welcome Back, Kotter* pal around together—an Italian, a black, a Puerto Rican Jew, a white eastern European ethnic—in a poverty-stricken neighborhood in Brooklyn where, in reality, racial polarization has been at a flash point for a decade or more. And they frequently arrive, alone or together, at the apartment of their teacher, an event which, for

A television wedding is a sure tonic for the ratings. In one of the gentlest of early situation comedies (below), Wally Cox as Mr. Peepers weds Patricia Benoit in 1954. Far left is Marion Lorne, a key supporting character. Not pictured is Tony Randall. In 1975, Rhoda (Valerie Harper) married Joe Gerard (David Groh) in a one-hour special (left) that won big ratings for CBS but sent the show off the tracks. A year later, Joe and Rhoda separated, and in the fall of 1977, they became divorced.

many New York teachers in such a neighborhood, would trigger an emergency call to the police. When Rhoda premiered on CBS in the fall of 1974, she was supposed to be a modern woman living alone; yet she moved into her sister's apartment. And when she was married off (under the push of then-CBS programming chief Fred Silverman, who wanted a ratings blockbuster), she managed to find an apartment in the same building as her sister. Even after its hit debut, Laverne & Shirley was changed to include the character of Laverne's father; a harassed, confused, but lovable pizza-parlor owner, he was an adult presence missing in the first season of the show.

So prevalent is the family in situation comedy that a stock opening line has become an industry joke as the symbol of the worn-out sit-com ("Hi, honey, I'm home!"). So concerned are producers and network programmers about preserving a family sensibility in the show that when sit-coms began to present one-parent families, the only safe explanation for the missing partner was death; divorce was considered unsettling. As late as 1975, NBC failed with Fay, a show about a vibrant woman in her forties who is in the process of discarding her husband and rediscovering her

Penny Marshall (left) as Laverne and Cindy Williams as Shirley are off on a frolic—disguised as men to erase their phone number scrawled on a men's room wall. Shortly after the hit series began in early 1976, Phil Foster arrived as Laverne's father to increase the show's "familial" quality.

Beneath the yelling, the screaming, the insults, and the imprecations are warm family ties. *All in the Family (left)*, the 1971 Norman Lear show that began the trend toward "realism" in sit-coms, binds (from left) Jean Stapleton (Edith Bunker), Sally Struthers (Gloria Stivic), Rob Reiner (Mike Stivic), and Carroll O'Connor (Archie Bunker), into a close family unit. If the kids hate the grownups, why are they living next door?

In *Good Times*, starring Esther Rolle (center) as Florida Evans, the father figure played by John Amos (right) embodied traditional middle-class values. When he was written out of the show because of a contract dispute, the family remained the focus of the show. One of the children, Thelma (BernNadette Stanis), is shown here.

own life and lusts. After two network airings, the show was canceled—in part because the network's research found audiences uncomfortable with the situation. Fay's estranged husband would often be a part of the setting, asking her to try again. As a comic device, the relationship between Lee Grant and Joe Silver often worked well; as a warm-hearted family arrangement, it was confusing, ambiguous. It did not work. (*One Day At a Time,* with a divorcee as the main character, has won good ratings, but here the woman lives with two teenage daughters.)

In contrast, consider the comedies of Norman Lear. Beginning with *All in the Family* and continuing through *Maude* and *Good Times,* Lear's comedies have often been called breakthroughs, and they have often used words and topics long considered taboo. Archie Bunker, the lead in Lear's first success, *All in the Family,* is a bigot who employs terms such as "black beauties" to describe blacks, "dagoes" for Italians, and similar expressions of nonendearment. From its debut, the show used the sexual appetite of the Bunkers' daughter and son-in-law for comic effect, and also devoted a show to the temporary impotence of the son-in-law. Edith Bunker went through menopause; a hero-athlete Archie knew turned out to be gay; a woman he encountered was really a transvestite male. Maude got pregnant and had an abortion; she and her husband went through a lengthy separation. The Evans family in *Good Times* lives in a Chicago housing project in the ghetto, and shows have touched on teenage alcoholism and the desperate efforts of the family to escape ceaseless poverty.

But the family ties in Norman Lear's comedies are thoroughly conventional, thoroughly middle American; they represent not a departure from the situation comedies of the past but an affirmation of the form. Archie Bunker is, in his own way, devoted to his wife and daughter and susceptible of emotional vulnerability (he is a far cry from his British inspiration, Alf Garnett of *Till Death Do Us Part,* whose bigotry, misogyny, and general meanness of spirit is mercilessly consistent). For all his fulminations against his "meathead" son-in-law, Mike and Gloria lived for years under the same roof as the Bunkers, and when they became parents of Archie's grandchild, they moved next door: not precisely the goal of a contemporary young couple of liberal political and sexual persuasion.

In *Good Times* and *The Jeffersons,* the fact that the principal characters are black is interesting, but not nearly as important as their embodiment of traditional values and their strong sense of family. Until the father figure in *Good Times,* played by John Amos, was killed off at the start of the 1976 season because of Amos's contractual dispute with Lear, the father was a powerful center of the family, with middle-class aspirations.

Beatrice Arthur and Bill Macy portray a modern, compulsively neurotic couple in *Maude;* he drinks, she screams, they fight, they even separate. But the family unit remains. The woman in the center is Hermione Baddeley, who plays the maid.

He was a strong parental presence, a dispenser of strict, corporal discipline; he insisted that his children stay in school, that they abide by the law. George Jefferson is the man who made it: an affluent man who dresses like a yacht club executive in his off-hours, he aspires to join the social elite, while his exasperated but loving wife reminds him of his ghetto origins. Both of these shows—in fact, all of Lear's network offerings—insist on the family as the source of strength and ethical values (*Mary Hartman, Mary Hartman* takes a more jaded view of home and hearth, which may be one reason why all three networks rejected it). And all of these shows, however precedent-shattering they are in confronting *issues,* resolve them with a return inward to the family. *Good Times* may be an ironic title given the characters' lifestyle of poverty, but the family is a center of warmth, love, and humor. As ABC's research vice-president, Marvin Mord, once observed, "the people in that show are *very happy* people."

Even in shows where the "family" is absent, the bond is very strong. *The Mary Tyler Moore Show* broke a lot of rules by presenting a young woman who lived alone, who was unmarried, and whose dates did not stop at the apartment door. Her parents were far away; there was no happy brood with whom she boarded.

In *The Mary Tyler Moore Show*, Mary's status as a single woman is balanced by the strong, familial ties at the office. She's shown *(left)* during a temporary spat with newswriter Murray Slaughter, played by Gavin MacLeod, with Ted Baxter (Ted Knight) in the middle.

This show, however, provided a familial bond through the workplace. Lou Grant, Murray Slaughter, even the laughable Ted Baxter were frequent visitors in each other's homes, and provided each other a shoulder to cry on, a hearing for grievances and pains. At home, there was Rhoda Morgenstern for sympathy and a dash of spice to counter Mary's originally sugary soul, and Phyllis Lindstrom for the vinegar (when Phyllis was spun off in her own show, Sue Ann Nivens, the "Happy Homemaker," was built up to provide the antidote of bitchiness to Mary's personality).

Sometimes the work family can erase the need for a more conventional family bond. In *Barney Miller*, the men (and token women) of the precinct house provide the tie; Barney Miller's wife became so irrelevant that she was written out of the show. And the ravages of war make a real family impossible on *M*A*S*H*; in-

stead, the company works as a family, from the fatherly colonel to the kid brother (Radar). No matter what the situation, no matter how independent they may seem, the show follows the unbreakable sit-com rule: do not leave these characters to face the world alone.

Aside from the standard requirement of a strong family composed of characters who will elicit audience involvement, situation comedy reflects another consistent pattern. What emerges is a kind of delayed-reaction portrayal of these familial bonds. Television life in situation comedy—not always, but often—reflects not "the way we live now," but the way we lived a few years ago. It's almost as if television in situation comedy is trying to put back into the American home those qualities that are no longer there; this is also true of dramatic series, in a different context, and especially true of television advertising.

Bob Newhart, playing a psychologist married to Suzanne Pleshette in *The Bob Newhart Show (left)*, cares for two "families"—the office crowd, and the childlike neighbor Howard (played by Bill Daily). ABC's *Barney Miller (below)* offers a close-knit unit of police detectives nicely spiced for ethnic diversity: "Wojo" (Maxwell Gail), Miller (Hal Linden), Harris (Ron Glass), Fish (Abe Vigoda), and Yemana (Jack Soo). Barbara Barrie, who played Miller's wife, was retired from the series, since she never really fit into the police "family."

A strong dose of ethnic characterizations found its way into early television shows via radio sit-coms, even as ethnic America was dispersing. Gertrude Berg's *The Goldbergs (top)* portrayed life in a loving Jewish home. Here, guest star Arthur Godfrey, center, surrounded by (from left) Eli Mintz, Arlene ("Fuzzy") McQuade, Larry Robinson, Gertrude Berg, and Philip Loeb, looks somewhat apprehensive as Molly Goldberg fills his plate. *I Remember Mama (center)*, starring Peggy Wood (far right), portrayed life in a loving Norwegian home. She shares a laugh here with the rest of the Hansen family— from left, Dick Van Patten, Judson Laire (as "Papa"), Robin Morgan, and Rosemary Rice. *Life with Father (bottom)*, adapted from the long-running Broadway show by Lindsay and Crouse, portrayed life in a loving WASP home. Leon Ames was Father (far left), and the family was played by (from left) Harvey Grant, Ralph Reed, Freddie Leiston, Ronald Keith, and Lurene Tuttle.

Television's early days, for example, brought to the screen a number of video versions of radio comedies dealing with the adventures of big-city ethnic families, with strong ties to Old World customs and values; the clash of values between the parents and the more sophisticated, more "Americanized" daughters and sons was a basic comedic theme of these shows. They were Italian *(Life With Luigi)*, Scandinavian *(I Remember Mama)*, Jewish *(The Goldbergs)*—and they were on television at the very time when, at the end of World War II, the rush to the suburbs was unraveling these kinds of families, beginning to drain the life and vitality from "the old neighborhoods."

The 1950s was a time when the "disappearing father" was a growing reality. In part because of the commuting distances between city and suburb, in part because of the movement into the white-collar class and the longer working hours that move required, in part because the small, family-owned and -operated shops were disappearing, the father figure was not home as often. And in the fifties there appeared—in contrast to popular nostalgic memory—not only the bumbling, ludicrous father image of Chester A. Riley (as played first by Jackie Gleason and then by William Bendix) or the amnesiac Stu Erwin in *Trouble with Father*, but a kind, concerned, and *ever-present* father. The laughs might be broad, as in Danny Thomas's *Make Room for Daddy* (later *The Danny Thomas Show*); they might be quiet, as in *Father Knows Best*; or they might be supplied wholly by a mechanical laugh track, as in *The Adventures of Ozzie and Harriet* (ABC's first successful situation comedy—and its only one for

Although fathers were spending less time at home in the late fifties, you'd never know it from these sit-coms. Danny Thomas, in *Make Room for Daddy*, later *The Danny Thomas Show (above)*, was frequently exasperated by his family, but he was always there to remind them of the proper moral principles, usually offered with the subtlety of a twenty-pound sledgehammer. Thomas is shown here with Angela Cartwright as his daughter, Marjorie Lord as his wife, Rusty Hamer as his son, and series regulars Pat Carroll and Sid Melton. Robert Young was the ever-calm father of *Father Knows Best (above, right)*, shepherding (on stairs, from left) Elinor Donahue, Billy Gray, and Lauren Chapin through life. Jane Wyatt played his wife. Raised voices? Violent family quarrels? No chance. Ozzie, Harriet *(right)*, Rick *(below)*, and Dave Nelson played—Ozzie, Harriet, Rick, and Dave, moving through life with the turbulence of a boat on a molasses-filled lake. What Ozzie did for a living was never divulged, but, based on his presence at home, the hours were right.

In these three examples of family comedy, the comedy was often all but invisible. In *My Three Sons (above, right),* Fred MacMurray played Steve Douglas, at first a widower, assisted by Uncle Charlie (William Demarest) in rearing his three sons, only one of whom, Chip (Barry Livingston), is pictured here, along with the second wife (Beverly Garland), Dodie (Dawn Lyn), and Tramp. "I'm worried about the Beaver, Ward," Barbara Billingsley said to Hugh Beaumont *(above, left)* in *Leave It to Beaver.* Why? Big brother Wally (Tony Dow) didn't even wear sideburns. If one "father" (Brian Keith) isn't enough, how about two? Sebastian Cabot played the ever-present Giles French in *A Family Affair (below),* a long-running CBS comedy. Johnny Whitaker, Anissa Jones, and Kathy Garver were their wards.

many years). But whatever the quality of the humor, these fathers were always there to listen to the problems of their children, to offer advice, to express concern ("I'm worried about the Beaver, Ward." "Mmmmm. Why?"). These men never seemed to be out of town or distracted by work pressures. In fact, it was impossible to figure out what Ozzie Nelson did at all besides sit in the living room waiting for Rick or David to come in with a domestic dilemma.

In the early 1960s, the American political tensions began to increase. The civil-rights movement began hitting the headlines; there were riots in New York City in 1964, fire hoses and police dogs in Birmingham, Alabama, in 1963 and in Selma, Alabama, in 1965. At first peacefully with sit-ins in 1961, then more divisively with Berkeley in 1964, signs that the younger generation was stirring appeared. During this time and throughout the later 1960s, the most successful string of situation comedies were CBS's rural, "hick" comedies, celebrating the values of small-town life. ABC actually began the form with *The Real McCoys* in 1957, starring Walter Brennan, Richard Crenna, and Kathleen Nolan as a family of self-reliant hillbillies. But it was *The Beverly Hillbillies*, featuring a family of mountain folk that struck it rich, moved to Beverly Hills, but kept its customs and values intact, that signaled the trend when it began on CBS in 1962. It is true, as David Boroff has written, that the show "offers the standard myths of populist reassurance: the superior wisdom of the unlettered; the fecklessness of the upper class, the gaiety of the ignorant, the pompous solemnity of the rich." It was in fact the city-slicker-bested-by-the-country-bumpkin routine.

Walter Brennan as grandpappy Amos and Richard Crenna as Luke *(above)* starred in the 1957 rural-comedy forerunner, *The Real McCoys*. The brood was big, fun-loving, and closely knit. Now take such a family, move them to corrupt, sophisticated Beverly Hills, preserve their traditions and simplicity, and what do you have? You have *The Beverly Hillbillies,* from 1962 to 1972 one of the most popular rural comedies *(top)*. Irene Ryan and Buddy Ebsen kept the younger members of the clan, Donna Douglas and Max Baer, in line.

The Andy Griffith Show, starring Griffith, Don Knotts, Ron Howard (later of *Happy Days*), and Frances Bavier, was another popular rural comedy, which spun off *Gomer Pyle—USMC* and *Mayberry R.F.D.*, perfect antidotes to the clamorous 1960s.

But it was also an escape route out of the increasingly difficult problems of discordant urban America. Along with its progeny—*Green Acres, The Andy Griffith Show, Petticoat Junction, Mayberry R.F.D.*—the show conjured up a way of life that did not require tranquilizers, that no urbanized black or civil-rights agitator could penetrate.

And during this same period in which America was growing quarrelsome with itself appeared another sitcom trend: the fantasy escape. *Bewitched, I Dream of Jeannie, My Favorite Martian, The Munsters, The Addams Family, My Mother the Car, My Living Doll, Mister Ed, Gilligan's Island* all began in the first half of the 1960s. All of them featured—through friendly ghouls, enchanted spells, or a fortuitous shipwreck—complete escape from the realities of American life.

The comedy that "broke the rules" of noncontroversial situation comedies, showing clashes between older and younger generations, between black and white, and between ethnic and WASP, did not air on CBS in the last half of the 1960s, when campuses and cities were in flames, when the war in Vietnam—and controversy over its handling—was at its peak. *All in the Family* had its premiere in January, 1971—when the passions were cooling down. Sometime between the Democratic National Convention of 1968 and the shootings at Kent State and Jackson State colleges in 1970, the tensions had erupted, then subsided. Only then—not when the divisiveness was strongest—could a comic treatment of still-existing serious divisions win mass audience acceptance.

Perhaps it takes time for writers, producers, and networks to absorb the currents in American life; perhaps they know, by instinct or by research, that it's important to let the currents ebb before presenting them in a comic frame of reference. Or perhaps ABC vice-president Bob Shanks, in his book *The Cool Fire*, explains why even out-of-phase reality works in comic, but not dramatic situations:

> We have been through the bruising sixties, when every issue was dragged kicking and screaming into the light, when every value, supposedly fixed in granite, was challenged and frequently seen to be made of chalk. . . . In the numbing and more resigned seventies, audiences know, and know that everybody else knows, what all the difficult, even insoluble problems are. What does one do in such cases? Laugh.
>
> What to make of all of this? If you are devising a drama, make it escapist; if you are creating a comedy, make it real . . . cartoon real.

(Shanks also predicted that silliness would soon be coming back; in the light of *Laverne & Shirley, Welcome*

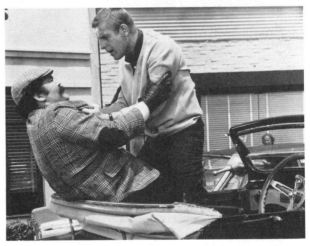

One of the earliest—and best—fantasy sit-coms was *Topper* (top, left), starring Leo G. Carroll as the stuffy Cosmo Topper, haunted by fun-loving ghosts Anne Jeffreys and Robert Sterling. *The Munsters (top, right),* a misunderstood family of ghouls, starred Yvonne De Carlo and Fred Gwynne. *My Mother the Car (bottom, right)* starred Jerry Van Dyke (right), here pictured with Avery Schreiber. Ann Sothern was the voice of Jerry's mother, reincarnated as an automobile. Alan Young *(bottom, left)* was the human friend of a talking horse in *Mister Ed.* The animal in *Bewitched (left, center)* is only visiting; Elizabeth Montgomery, the star, is shown with Maurice Evans.

Another handy route to escape is to maroon your characters on a desert island. Bob Denver (front, wearing a sailor cap) was Gilligan, supported by (from left) Russell Johnson, Alan Hale, Dawn Wells, Tina Louise, Jim Backus, and Natalie Schafer. *Gilligan's Island* is often ranked with *My Mother the Car* in the annals of absurd situation comedies.

Don Adams (right) as Maxwell Smart, Agent 86, and Barbara Feldon as Agent 99 confront "The Chief," played by Edward C. Platt, in *Get Smart!,* a parody of the James Bond genre that surfaced in dramatic television shows of the 1960s. This show, created by Buck Henry and Mel Brooks, sent several catchphrases into the culture: "Sorry about that" and "Would you believe...?" among them.

Besides the obvious use of the familial ties such a life enforces, how is the military treated in situation comedy? In *You'll Never Get Rich (bottom),* a brilliant writing team headed by the late Nat Hiken and a brilliant cast headed by Phil Silvers (shown here along with Harvey Lembeck, second from left, Maurice Gosfield, far right, and other members of Company B) created some of the finest sit-com moments. In *Hogan's Heroes (below),* Allied prisoners of war in World War II, led by Bob Crane, foreground, played Dead End Kids to laughable Nazis (Werner Klemperer, left, Cynthia Lyn, and John Banner); the premise unsettled many. *Gomer Pyle—USMC (right)* starred Jim Nabors and Frank Sutton in a show that, in its attempt to avoid any social comment, succeeded admirably.

Back, Kotter, and other ABC comic offerings, this prediction makes him a prophet with honor at his own network.)

None of these points is to deny the skills that can make a television comedy as funny as a good Broadway show. The old Phil Silvers show, *You'll Never Get Rich,* featuring Sgt. Bilko's platoon pitted against the bureaucratic Colonel Hall, produced several comic gems. One of them, "The Court Martial," about a chimpanzee mistakenly inducted into the army during a manic attempt at efficiency, is a classic satire on bureaucracy. The first *Dick Van Dyke Show,* created by Carl Reiner and featuring the first-rate comic cast of Van Dyke, Mary Tyler Moore, Morey Amsterdam, and Rose Marie, was a flawlessly played light comedy. Many of Lear's shows, and those of MTM Productions, work as entertainment and as often touching character sketches. In particular, *The Mary Tyler Moore Show* bent the immobile character forms: Lou Grant, the newsroom boss, lost his wife to divorce and remarriage; he became, in the words of one of the show's creators, "a casualty of the feminist revolution." Mary became more assertive, less the country girl lost in the big city. *M*A*S*H,* the bittersweet comedy set in the Korean War, has proved that the sit-com form can not only be bent, but also broken, provided the audience knows what the situation is (men and women under siege), and who the characters are. The show has often dropped the element of "comedy" completely, dealing instead with the horror of young men dying in combat. Sometimes there is no "situation," only a series of vignettes as recounted by Hawkeye in his letters home. In one episode, built around the premise of an American television reporter interviewing the people of the MASH unit, the entire show was shot in black-and-white—as it would have appeared on television in the early

M*A*S*H, which began in 1972, broke many of the rules of situation comedies. By maintaining a high level of writing and acting, and by having the good sense to link a brilliant actor (Alan Alda as Hawkeye) with a brilliant executive producer-director (Larry Gelbart), *M*A*S*H* became the most honest and outspoken of all situation comedies. The original cast featured (front row, from left) Wayne Rogers as Trapper, Alan Alda as Hawkeye, McLean Stevenson as Colonel Henry Blake, and Gary Burghoff as Radar. In rear are "Hot Lips" Houlihan (Loretta Swit) and Major Frank Burns (Larry Linville).

Two examples of early sit-com stereotyping are shown here. In *My Little Margie (left)*, Gale Storm played a scatterbrained adult woman who bedeviled her father (Charles Farrell, left); her brains were matched by those of her boyfriend Freddie (Don Hayden). In *Beulah (right)*, a succession of black actresses—this one is Louise Beavers (left), pictured with Ruby Dandridge—showed how happy life as a domestic could be.

1950s—and the actors improvised their responses to the questions, talking about fear and anger and horror under the conditions of war.

It is also clearly true that situation comedy today is not simply more realistic about topics, but also about people. The comedies of the first twenty years of commercial television—almost without exception—were monolithic in their representation of prevailing cultural values. Women stayed at home or worked in role-defined jobs such as secretary, teacher, and model; and while millions of women were entering the work force in the 1950s and 1960s, television treated the idea that a woman might go to work while a man stayed home and cared for the children as a comic device. People, particularly the women of such shows as *I Love Lucy* and *My Little Margie*, were children—manipulative, lying, deceptive, constitutionally unable to say to husband or father, "I know you're bringing the boss home for dinner, but I burned the roast, so let's go out to eat." Instead, twenty-one minutes of deception was required. Blacks in those television shows were either invisible or played as complete stereotypes: Willie Best

portrayed the bug-eyed elevator operator on *My Little Margie*, Ethel Waters (and Hattie McDaniel and Louise Beavers) played the happy-go-lucky domestic on *Beulah*, and not until the 1968 airing of *Julia* on NBC did a network cast a black as a leading figure (though how the character, ostensibly a nurse, could afford an apartment and wardrobe more suitable to a corporate vice-president was never explained).

Situation comedy today is in *its* "golden age." It is more honest and funnier than it has ever been, and gives a more accurate portrayal of American life than do most serious shows. What this suggests is that the viewing audience is prepared to accept some unpleasant or divisive topics—provided the context itself is comfortable and relatively reassuring. Once we know that these characters are endearing (despite their prejudices or shortcomings), once we know that they are safe from the ravages of loneliness and abandonment, once we know that they are protected by the kinds of roots most Americans seem to be longing for, we can laugh with them and cry with them, secure in their own warm, protective familial bond.

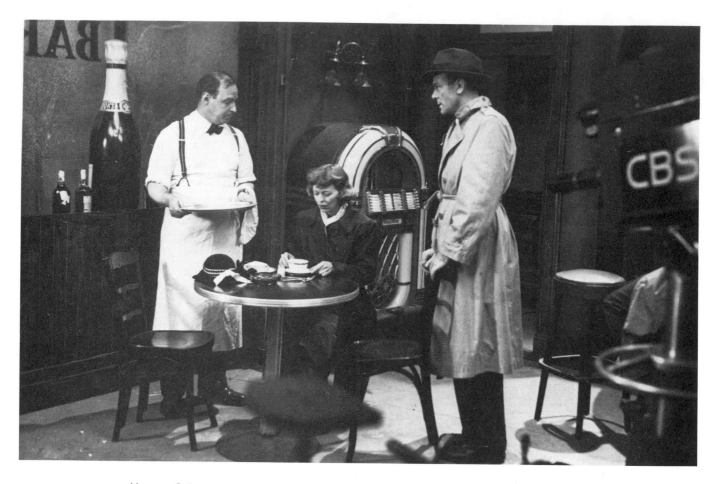

Margaret Sullavan starred in *The Storm* in 1948, the first production of *Studio One*, a CBS weekly anthology drama. *The Last Cruise*, a 1950 *Studio One* production, ventured to create visual excitement within the cramped limits of the studio.

DRAMA
AND ADVENTURE

Despite the enormous strides in technology which have considerably enlarged television's capabilities, many of the program forms of television have remained remarkably constant over the last thirty years. The early morning news shows, the late-night and midday talk shows, the network news, game shows, soap operas, and situation comedies—all have retained their essential shapes. The one television form that has changed almost completely from television's early days is the dramatic form.

It has changed production location: from New York to Los Angeles. It has changed texture: from live television to film. It has changed format: from the "anthology" series, presenting original works and dramatic adaptations covering a wide range of topics, to the continuing series, featuring characters whose vocations, surroundings, companions, and emotional responses are rigidly defined. (While these series have been supplemented over the last decade with the made-for-TV movie and the more recent concept of the "mini-series," continuing series are still the bedrock offerings of network television in the dramatic range.) It has changed content: from closeup emotional conflict emphasizing character, best suited to live, studio-originated shows, to physical conflict emphasizing action—fists, guns, cars, and explosives—best suited to film.

The reasons for these changes—a mix of economics, network competitiveness, advertising pressure, popular taste, and corporate timidity—tell much about the way the shape of television itself has changed since its introduction into American life almost thirty years ago. They also point to a structural conflict that is rooted in the very existence of a commercial broadcasting system: it is licensed by the government to serve the public interest, but operated by a cluster of private interests working to earn the biggest possible profit from a medium that cannot be expanded beyond the absolute limits of time.

The early days of television were characterized by conditions that helped to create the climate for a wide variety of relatively freewheeling television drama. First, all production originated in New York City, because that is where the headquarters of radio broadcasting were located, and that is where the networks established

their experimental television studios: CBS in a Grand Central Station studio, NBC on the third floor of 30 Rockefeller Plaza. This meant that, by geographic proximity alone, the influence on television drama in the early days came from Broadway rather than Hollywood. The movie studios, in fact, regarded television as a mortal enemy, and refused to have anything to do with it during its first few years.

Second, in the late 1940s television was not truly a "mass medium." Even as late as 1950, only 4.4 million television sets had been purchased in America; the coaxial cable, permitting live television transmission across great distances, did not reach Chicago until 1949, and Los Angeles until 1951; many communities, especially in the mountain and western states, did not have access to television; and the initial high price of receivers made it at first a plaything of the relatively affluent. Nor were those first few years a source of great profit: through 1948, NBC was losing $13,000 a day on television. On the other hand, advertising rates were low: the same hour of studio time that cost $27,215 on network radio cost $1,510 on television. There was thus not much to lose in producing offbeat drama, either in terms of offending great masses or in risking huge amounts of money. And the very lack of alternatives, the dependence on live, studio production, made the dramatic play the most feasible form to present on television.

However much contemporary network programmers like to disparage "the Golden Age of television drama," however true it is that many of these early offerings were amateurishly written, directed, and acted, the fact is that television drama through the first decade of its existence was, by present standards, astonishingly diverse. It began in May of 1947, with the premiere of *The Kraft Television Theatre* on NBC. It flourished with no less than eleven network anthology shows every week in the early 1950s, including *Studio One, The Philco-Goodyear Playhouse, The United States Steel Hour, Robert Montgomery Presents, Playhouse 90* (the only weekly entry to originate from California). It was buttressed by a series of less frequent dramatic shows: *Du Pont Show of the Month, The Hallmark Hall of Fame,* the frequent dramatic presentations on *Omnibus*. Its es-

Du Pont Show of the Month provided outstanding dramas in the late 1950s. This production of *Wuthering Heights* in 1958 starred Richard Burton, Denholm Elliott (rear), and Yvonne Furneaux (shortly before the live airing of the show, she was replaced by Rosemary Harris).

The Hollywood-based *Playhouse 90* attempted to preserve the New York tradition of live, original dramas. Its second show, Rod Serling's *Requiem for a Heavyweight (extreme left)*, was an outstanding production, starring Jack Palance, Keenan Wynn, and his father Ed Wynn. *Days of Wine and Roses (far left)*, a *Playhouse 90* original production written by J. P. Miller, starred Cliff Robertson, Piper Laurie, and Charles Bickford (not shown). In 1958, the show adapted Irwin Shaw's *Eighty-Yard Run (left)*, into a drama starring Paul Newman (right) and Joanne Woodward, shown here with Richard Anderson.

One of the most ambitious efforts to program for a frankly "elitist" audience resulted in *Omnibus*, hosted by Alistair Cooke. The show appeared on each of the three commercial networks successively from 1952 to 1959. Here Cooke introduces the Broadway cast of *Oklahoma!*

In 1959, *Playhouse 90* mounted an expensive ($300,000) two-part taped production of Hemingway's *For Whom the Bell Tolls,* starring Jason Robards, Jr., and Maria Schell. It was a brave but futile attempt to preserve anthology drama as a regular feature of commercial television.

sential content, as one student of television, William Bluem, put it, "was anthology drama—stories of human conflict and confrontation, played with honesty and authority in living sight, sound, and motion before audiences the size of which no actor, writer, or director in all theatrical history would have dared to dream." There were, to be sure, times when the producers and directors of these early series sought to experiment with the limits of studio television. In 1956, *The Kraft Television Theatre* staged *A Night to Remember,* about the sinking of the *Titanic*, which required 107 actors, 31 sets, and 7 cameras. In 1959, when anthology drama was beginning to decline, *Playhouse 90* spent the then incredible sum of $300,000 for a taped, two-part version of *For Whom the Bell Tolls*. Essentially, however, television drama was small-scale, tightly contained in space and scope, technically incapable of incorporating, for example, car chases, exploding warehouses, and chases down city streets. The focus had to be on people: what they said, what they thought, what they feared. And because television combined the closeup possibilities of film with the intangible magic of a live, this-is-it performance, television drama was able, as *Hallmark Hall of Fame* producer George Schaefer put it, "to catch the glowing, growing kind of performance you might see on the stage if you were a bumblebee buzzing around everywhere you wanted to be. This is a distinct contribution of television. In this unique way, the medium does something beyond the living stage, and something film can't do at all."

In sheer quantity, the live dramatic output of television was staggering. One study estimated that between 1950 and 1955, for just *three* weekly series, more than three hundred original hour-long plays were written and produced. These were not scripts written to order, based on preexisting characters, conflicts, or problems; they were plays written because the writer had something to say, and had an outlet where he was permitted to say it. As to quality, TV historians Arthur Shulman and Roger Youman, in their book *How Sweet It Was*, found that for one week in the fall of 1954 "one could see: 'Middle of the Night,' with E. G. Marshall and Eva Marie Saint; 'Twelve Angry Men,' with Franchot Tone; an adaptation of 'Lady in the Dark,' starring Ann Sothern; a play by Robert E. Sherwood . . . and a half-dozen others—all live, of course . . . " They found much the same pattern in 1955. And the measure of achievement is to be found less in the occasional spectacular triumph—Paddy Chayefsky's *Marty* with Rod Steiger and Nancy Marchand, Reginald Rose's *Twelve Angry Men*, Rod Serling's *Patterns*—than in the fact that every week there was room for the likes of Chayefsky, Rose, Serling, Tad Mosel, Robert Alan Aurthur, Gore Vidal, Calder Willingham, and other young, unknown writers.

The anthologies also employed such directors as John Frankenheimer, Sidney Lumet, and George Roy Hill. Nor were these shows confined to an Eastern intellectual ghetto; as late as December, 1954, four of the ten top-rated shows were weekly anthology dramas.

What happened to the age of live, character-based, small-scale anthology drama? Television began to change as the medium began to grow and absorb everything in its path—especially its onetime rivals, the movie studios. Technology, economics, and simple fear combined to all but obliterate a once crucial element of commercial television.

First, look at some of the disadvantages of live television in the early days. The most obvious disadvantage was that it was a one-time-only proposition. For each week new sets, new costumes, new props were required. And as television costs grew, those expenses grew more burdensome. And since the technology of videotape recording was not perfected until the early 1960s, these performances could be preserved only on kinescope: a grainy, technically imperfect and nonmarketable film shot off a television screen. There was no way to "print up" several hundred copies of a brilliant show and sell it to independent stations, theaters, and foreign markets. In fact, when shows such as *Patterns* were met with acclaim and were repeated, the entire production had to be mounted again from scratch.

Second, the early days of television were marked by far more sponsor control of programming than was the case after the late 1950s. Sponsors had their names on many of the programs (*Alcoa Theatre, The Philco-Goodyear Playhouse, The Kraft Television Theatre*). They were, with few exceptions, hostile to controversy, fearful of it. One reason for the success of the television blacklist was the unsubtle threat of economic retaliation against sponsors of shows using "disloyal" talent. The most famous case involved Laurence Johnson, an upstate New York supermarket owner and prime supporter of Aware, Incorporated, a private investigative group which published *Red Channels* and *Counterattack*, whose lists of "infiltrators" were authoritative to the blacklisters. Johnson threatened uncooperative advertisers with damaging public attack. He promised to display their products in his supermarkets under signs alleging, in effect, that they were manufactured by companies that supported Communist-leaning entertainers. And he vowed to help spread this device to stores outside his control. The threat was often enough to force advertisers into cooperation with the blacklisters. But beyond this, sponsors in the days of early television were fearful that the medium's power was such that any connection between a sponsor and an unpleasantry would poison the mind of the consumer against the sponsor. Erik Barnouw provides endless

This 1955 NBC *Producers' Showcase* production starred Henry Fonda, Lauren Bacall (far left), and Humphrey Bogart (back to camera, far right), among others, in a live television version of *Petrified Forest,* Robert E. Sherwood's classic drama.

Frank Sinatra (right) was the Stage Manager and Paul Newman and Eva Marie Saint the principals in this television adaptation of Thornton Wilder's *Our Town,* staged in 1955 for *Producers' Showcase.*

In 1954, *Studio One* presented an original script, Reginald Rose's *Twelve Angry Men*. Taking full advantage of the inherent limits of live studio drama, it was an intense character study of men under pressure, starring Franchot Tone (seated, center), Robert Cummings, Edward Arnold, and Paul Hartman (clustered together, rear center). It later became a successful film starring Henry Fonda and Ed Begley.

examples of sponsor interference: a Ford Motor Company functionary ordering the Chrysler Building painted out of the New York City skyline; cigarette manufacturers insisting that all heroes, and no villains, smoke cigarettes in their programs; the American Gas Association forcing deletion of the word "gas" in a *Playhouse 90* show, *Judgment at Nuremberg*, thus making it sound as though six million Jews perished in "———— chambers."

A Procter & Gamble memorandum of the 1950s instructed its television time buyers more broadly. "There will," it said, "be no material that may give offense, either directly or by inference, to any commercial organization of any sort . . . There will be no material on any of our programs which could in any way further the concept of business as cold, ruthless, or lacking all sentiment or spiritual motivation."

With live television drama, the sponsor faced a potential battle with a writer and a director every single week. There might be a script about a black family trying to move into the suburbs (changed, under pressure, to an exconvict); there might be attacks on the criminal justice system, as in *Twelve Angry Men*, or on corporate infighting, as in *Patterns*, or even on television itself, as in *The Velvet Alley*. On live television, an actor might get carried away, as happened one Sunday in a *Philco*

Playhouse drama on bigotry, where an actor screamed at a mob, "You goddamn bullies and pigs!" There was, in short, no corporate security.

In fairness, it must be said that advertisers were far from the only fearful purveyors of mass culture in the 1950s. The Hollywood community had been the first to blacklist leftist writers, actors, and directors. Adhering to its own Production Code, Hollywood presented a view of social and sexual conduct that was rampantly dishonest: straying from the path of heterosexual monogamy required divine punishment; married couples slept in twin beds with enough garments to warm an Eskimo; and the makers of a 1953 movie, *The Moon Is Blue,* fought a pitched battle with censors because, among other things, it contained the words "virgin" and "pregnant." Even in the literary world, the cultural climate of the 1950s was very different; for example, the unexpurgated edition of *Lady Chatterley's Lover* could not be legally sold. In the world of movies and books, however, it was—is—always possible for some maverick to break with the prevailing rules, to risk a legal liability, to force the mainstream a bit wider. Should a broadcaster or a sponsor find himself embroiled in controversy, there are a raft of consequences that might follow. A government regulatory agency can remind stations that they exist as federal licensees (for a period in the 1950s, the Federal Communications Commission had a member, John Doerfer, handpicked by Senator Joseph McCarthy); interest groups can pressure sponsors by boycotting their products; sponsors, in turn, could, in the 1950s, pull their advertising from a program, forcing the network to continue it at a loss, or pull it from the schedule. (Today, with sponsors no longer controlling program content or network schedules, such a threat has far less impact.) In a time of uncertainty and fear, corporate advertising—the lifeblood of commercial television—could not accept the sometimes downbeat, sometimes dissenting view of American culture and society presented by many anthology dramas.

There was, however, an even more important element in the decline and fall of original network television drama, one that had its roots in the effort of a junior network to build toward equality with NBC and CBS. NBC was the first broadcasting network, organized in 1926. A year later, United Independent Broadcasters was formed, which soon became CBS. By the 1930s, the two networks were roughly competitive, though it took the "theft" of Jack Benny from NBC in the late 1940s to give CBS its first edge over NBC. (Aptly enough, considering Benny's carefully nurtured image as a miser, CBS won him over by offering him a complex tax-shelter deal to increase his wealth.) But the American Broadcasting Company was a perennial stepchild. It had begun op-

Disneyland opened in 1955, a year after Walt Disney began producing a weekly show for ABC, *Disneyland.* Its popularity convinced the other movie studios to go into television production—a move that pulled television west and spelled the end of live, New York-based dramas.

erations with NBC's weaker "blue" network as its foundation in 1943, with virtually no capital, no reputation, no tradition. Its so-called television "network" was virtually nonexistent in the first years of postwar television, and although *The Kraft Television Theatre* split its week between NBC and ABC in 1953 and 1954, the fledgling network had no dramatic offerings of consequence.

A Supreme Court antitrust ruling in 1948 that movie studios must divest themselves of their theater holdings forced Paramount to split into two companies—Paramount Pictures Corporation and United Paramount Theaters. Looking for a new partner, United Paramount Theaters turned to ABC. In 1953, the merger was completed, and its architect, Leonard Goldenson, took control of the new corporation. By training, by instinct, and in desperation, he turned to Hollywood as a possible source of network programming. While every major studio remained adamantly opposed to producing for television, Goldenson did find his first opening with Walt Disney. In return for the right to plug his movies on the television show and a healthy chunk of ABC investment for his new California amusement park, Disney agreed to supply a weekly show. The *Disneyland* series premiered in 1954 and quickly became the most popular show in the country. More important for the future of television, it convinced the major movie studios that

After the success of Walt Disney, Warner Brothers entered the television production field with a series of programs made for the ABC-TV network. Most successful of the first group was *Cheyenne*, starring Clint Walker as frontier scout Cheyenne Bodie.

television might be a profitable partner of films instead of its nemesis.

It was Warner Brothers that broke the ranks of the "majors" by producing for ABC—also in return for the right to plug its films at the end of the shows—a series of filmed adventures called *Warner Bros. Presents*. The series of rotating shows, which began in 1955, included *King's Row, Cheyenne* (the most popular of the first group), and *Colt .45*. Later in the 1950s they offered such successful adventure series as *77 Sunset Strip*. The important thing, however, was that the Hollywood studios began to flock to television as a means of finding work for idle sound stages, cameras, technicians, actors, and producers. And suddenly the full financial dimensions of the filmed series began to strike home. The new product was *film*—it could be run one time or fifty; it could be rerun with virtually no cost save the projectionist (later the computer operator); it could be sold to independent stations once the network was tired of the show; it could be sold abroad. It was a source of endless profit, as opposed to a one-shot item.

The filmed series had another advantage as well: it was *safe*. Once a show took the form of a regular dramatic series with a continuing set of principal characters, the headache of a weekly battle between writer, producer, director, sponsor, and network was considerably lessened. A network could shape the dimensions of a show even before it went on the air; it could test the concept by showing a pilot to audiences, demographically selected and scientifically monitored, to see what characters they liked, what settings excited them. By definition, this was impossible with live, original drama, since an audience could not make a judgment until the show was telecast. Further, live anthology drama had no continuing, sympathetic, attractive character to keep an audience tuned in at the same time every week. This was becoming increasingly important to networks, since, under pressure from the networks, which sought total control over their scheduling, the sponsors were abandoning direct programming. A company might happily sponsor a prestigious show, even if it did not win high ratings, for its own purposes: to project good will, or to reach a select audience. But as the networks took over total control of choosing the shows that went on the air, it became essential to maximize the audience at every hour of every day, since it was now numbers—not a select time slot—that determined how high the advertising rates went. (For their part, advertisers were finding distinct advantages in scattering their ads across network schedules, instead of risking everything on the hope that an audience might watch its one or two "big" shows.)

The networks were looking for predictability—for the

An example of television's ability to create appealing characters is found in *77 Sunset Strip,* an early Warner Brothers ABC drama. The ostensible star was Efrem Zimbalist, Jr., but the attention went to Edd Byrnes as the hair-combing "Kookie" (he's shown here with Sue Randall). The character inspired the hit song, "Kookie, Kookie, Lend Me Your Comb."

In *The Millionaire*, Michael Anthony (played by Marvin Miller) worked for the eccentric billionaire John Beresford Tipton, who dropped a million dollars a week (tax-free) into the laps of unsuspecting folks (here Frank McHugh plays the beneficiary) to see how they would react. The show spawned fantasies the nation over.

A pioneer in writing anthology drama, Rod Serling became disenchanted with television when anthologies died out. He became the host of *Twilight Zone*, a popular fantasy anthology of the early 1960s, and then of *Night Gallery*. Serling was also prominent in commercials. He died of a heart ailment in 1975.

The Outer Limits, a fantasy anthology of the 1960s, featured the scariest monsters ever seen on television. Here (from left) Jay Novello, Jerry Douglas, Ralph Meeker, and Henry Silva examine an unusual catch.

This champion of regular weekly series featured the brave, stoic hero in constant jeopardy. Marshal Dillon (James Arness, right) spent eighteen years fighting evil, assisted by the gimpy but game Chester (Dennis Weaver) and the hard-boiled but soft-hearted saloon hostess, Kitty (Amanda Blake).

security attending the knowledge that every Tuesday night at 8 P.M. an audience tuned in Milton Berle, or that every Monday night at 9 P.M. *I Love Lucy* appeared. Anthology dramas might light up the numbers one week and sag the next. And the costs of those by now antiquated New York studios were becoming impossible. CBS had already begun the move to California in 1956 by telecasting *Playhouse 90* from its new Television City broadcast center—a center built with TV in mind, eliminating the horrendous cost of building, disassembling, transporting, and reassembling sets in New York while dealing with a dozen different craft unions in the process.

So by the late 1950s, Hollywood was the place; the dramatic series was the form; repetition was the key; predictability was the goal. In 1963, with regular weekly anthology dramas all but extinct, and with the series form taking a firm foothold in the network schedules, two Golden Age veterans, Franklin Schaffner, producer-director of *Du Pont Show of the Month*, and Lewis Freedman of *Play of the Week*, recognized basic facts about these dramas that would remain constant over the next fifteen years.

Schaffner talked of "the essential difference between

the East Coast and West Coast writer. An East Coast writer comes in, sits down, and says . . . 'I've got an idea.' Then he tells you his story. A West Coast writer comes in, sits down, and says . . . 'What do you want me to write?' "

Freedman noted that "the 'fiction' we talk of has moved away from a conflict of psychology or character, or a conflict of morality, to a conflict of *action*, and that's why we've had the move to film—because film is the best medium for activity. 'Live' TV and the theatre are better suited to a static form in which the action is *interior*."

Schaffner also noted that a viewer accustomed to series drama, with its sudden bursts of action, would find anthology drama increasingly difficult to accept.

"He watches for a minute and a half," he said, "and begins to look at the clock because nobody has been killed yet. No woman is mangled. No child is in terrible danger. Then he rutches around in his seat, and all of a sudden, he's not listening. And if there's any literate quality to the script, he's *got* to be listening."

The American television audience, however, apparently wanted to listen to other fare: to the action-oriented, good-guy-bad-guy format which the

Wanted—Dead or Alive (above), circa 1960, was distinguished primarily by its star, Steve McQueen (right), shown here with Arthur Hunnicut. In *Rawhide (top, left)*, another future movie star, Clint Eastwood (left, shown with Eric Fleming), helped make the West safe for everyone but Indians. *Bat Masterson (left),* starring Gene Barry (shown with Adele Mara), was a really *different* western. See, he carried a *stick* instead of a gun, and…

In *Have Gun—Will Travel (opposite page, top)*, Richard Boone as Paladin anticipated the James Bond craze with his portrayal of an elegant, sophisticated private agent working for money, not for a government.

A western motif for the spy fad of the mid-1960s was employed in *Wild, Wild West (opposite page, bottom)*. Robert Conrad and Ross Martin (behind bars, right) played secret agents for President Grant. Here they are prisoners of the notorious Dr. Lovelace, played by Michael Dunn (foreground), supported by Phoebe Dorin.

Hollywood-produced series presented. They came in fads: *Gunsmoke*, carried over from the successful radio drama in 1955, and starring James Arness as the John Wayne–style Marshal Dillon, was for years one of the most popular shows in America. It triggered a spate of western series. By 1959 there were more than thirty regularly scheduled westerns on television every week. In that year, all of the top three shows and five of the top ten were westerns. "You know what differentiated them?" former CBS programming chief Mike Dann once recalled. "The size of the *gun*. Steve McQueen [in *Wanted: Dead or Alive*] had a sawed-off shotgun. Chuck Connors [*The Rifleman*] had a rifle. Paladin [protagonist of *Have Gun—Will Travel*] put a revolver in a holster with a chess knight on it."

The fads and trends kept changing. There were "quirky cop" fads—law enforcement types with odd foibles. Cannon was fat; Longstreet was blind; Columbo was outwardly sloppy; Barnaby Jones was a "countrified Columbo," according to his creator. There were "empire westerns" featuring tightly knit families of dynastic scope. *Bonanza* triggered that fad; *The High Chaparral*, *The Virginian*, and others followed suit. There were repeated cycles of doctor shows, from the early *Medic* to *Ben Casey* and *Doctor Kildare* to *Marcus Welby, M.D.* and *Medical Center*. There were endless

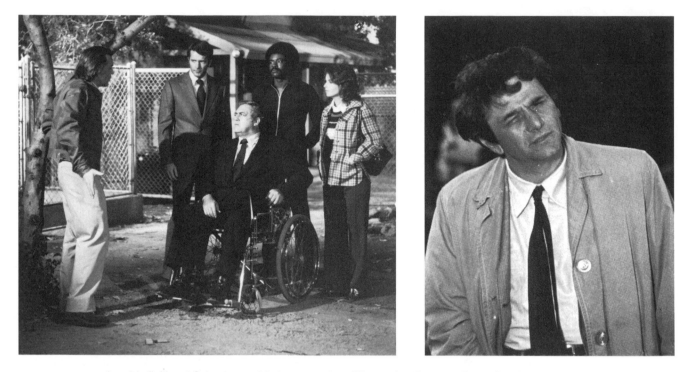

Ironside (left) and *Columbo* provide two examples of "humanized" police officers. San Francisco police chief Ironside, played by Raymond Burr, was crippled by a sniper's bullet and confined to a wheelchair. (Burr is shown here with loyal aides played by Don Galloway, behind Burr, and Don Mitchell. Elizabeth Baur is at far left.) Columbo, portrayed fetchingly by Peter Falk, is a sloppy, blood-fearing cop with a working-class background who undoes the (always) wealthy, powerful criminal.

James Drury (left, shown here with Sara Lane and Don Quine), starred in *The Virginian*. This NBC western was the first regular series to break the one-hour convention and appear as a long-form (ninety-minute) drama.

Bonanza—the ultimate family western. Lorne Greene (center) reigned as Ben Cartwright, patriarch of the Ponderosa Ranch (roughly the size of western Europe), shown here with his sons Hoss (Dan Blocker, left) and Little Joe (Michael Landon). So tightly knit was this family that the threat of the family being separated by a son's romance had to be met by divine intervention: the girl died.

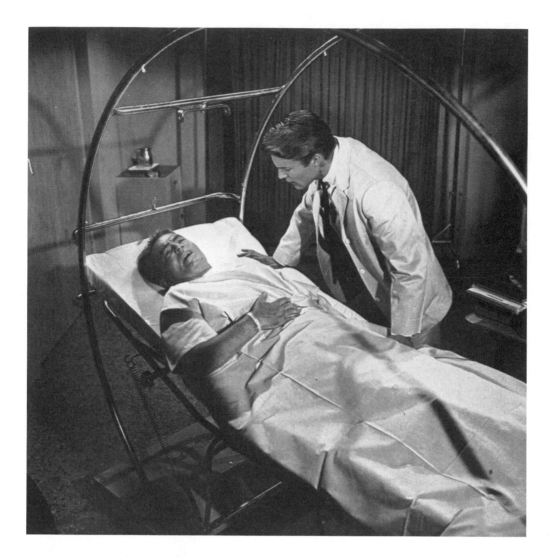

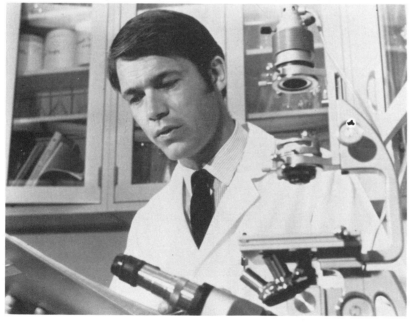

Because doctors hold the power of life and death in their hands, they are natural heroes for dramatic series. In *Dr. Kildare (above)* Richard Chamberlain was the idealistic young intern in a series adapted from the movie hits. Chad Everett as Joe Gannon on *Medical Center (left)* found that personal and emotional crises inevitably accompanied the physical problems of patients who came into his care.

Lawyers, like doctors, are credible series heroes because they work with people whose lives are in crisis. In *Perry Mason (left),* Raymond Burr bested D.A. Hamilton Burger (William Talman) week after week—with this one exception—by inducing dramatic courtroom confessions. An exceptional series was *The Defenders,* which aired on CBS in the early sixties. It featured a father-and-son team played by E. G. Marshall (at bench in middle) and Robert Reed (seated, right), who took on highly sensitive issues—censorship, capital punishment, blacklisting, abortion. Here they oppose J. D. Cannon (left), who later appeared as a harassed police captain on *McCloud.*

lawyer shows. Raymond Burr as *Perry Mason* was the most durable; Reginald Rose's *The Defenders*, starring E. G. Marshall and Robert Reed, was the most distinguished. There were old, crusty, but lovable cops teamed with young, idealistic, naïve, but lovable cops; old, crusty, but lovable doctors teamed with young, idealistic, naïve, but lovable doctors.

But beyond the names and trends are the characteristics that defined the overwhelming majority of these shows, and so severely limited them in their dramatic range. First, the shows required audience empathy with the principal. In his master's thesis, a young graduate student noted of ABC's action shows of the late 1950s that "each . . . has a leading man with whom the audience can easily identify. They are all distinct personalities—flesh and blood characters who possess an intangible quality which makes them real and believable." (This student, named Fred Silverman, became the head of CBS programming at the age of thirty-two. Five years later, he became the programming chief of ABC and pulled it into prime-time dominance for the first time in the network's history.) The search for audience empathy helps explain the producers' and programmers' ceaseless search for some kind of "humanizing" quality

A bright lad, a brighter dog, danger, rescue; it's been surefire for forty years. In this episode of *Lassie*, Jan Clayton reads a note as Tommy Rettig looks on. Lassie corrects the spelling.

Lloyd Bridges was frequently all wet and so were many of the plots, but *Sea Hunt* contained exceptional underwater photography.

In a classic dramatic formula, two attractive young men (George Maharis, left, and Martin Milner) travel around the country in their Corvette, finding action, adventure, and romance. *Route 66* provided a mix of escape, involvement, and freedom that appealed to the homebound viewer.

to offset the totally predictable nature of the plots faced by the hero. If Raymond Burr is to play a tough police chief in *Ironside*, make him a cripple in a wheelchair to give him a touch of humanity. If Telly Savalas must play a tough police chief battling the dregs of New York underworld life in *Kojak*, then make the audience sit up and take notice of his habit of sucking lollipops—a childlike quirk for such a tough man. Even when a character is required to *not* express emotion—as Matt Dillon was in *Gunsmoke*—he should be surrounded by colorful, "quirky" friends—as Matt Dillon was, with the limping, faithful Chester (Dennis Weaver), the hard-boiled but engaging Kitty (Amanda Blake), the crusty, folk-wise Doc (Milburn Stone).

Second, these characters *must* be involved in a larger-than-life enterprise, one that places life-or-death questions in their hands, if not subjecting them to life-or-death danger, every week. Michael Eisner, who used

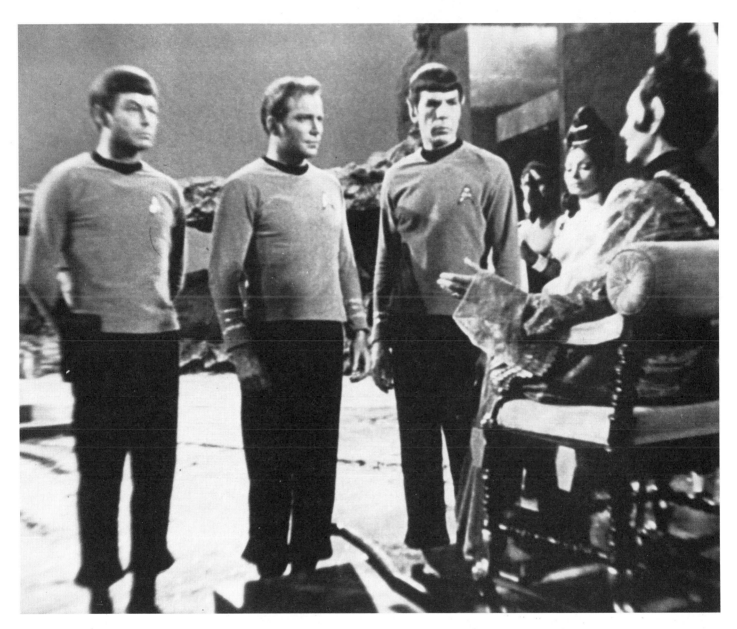

Star Trek, which aired on NBC for 3 years and was saved from cancellation in 1967–68 by one of the largest outpourings of viewer mail in television history, still has a large, passionate following. The crew of the starship U.S.S. *Enterprise* (Leonard Nimoy, William Shatner, and DeForest Kelley, from left) was aided by occasional scripts of the highest science-fiction caliber. Gene Roddenberry was the creator and executive producer of the show.

Paul Michael Glaser (as Starsky, left) and David Soul play the leads in *Starsky and Hutch*, a typical dramatic formula show. They are good buddies, they make their own rules, they drive a distinctive car, they shoot guns, they save each other's lives, they chase bad guys very fast in their distinctive car, they get hurt, they don't die, they always get their man...

to run West Coast programming operations for ABC and then became head of television production with Paramount, explains that "it's very difficult to find twenty-four stories to spend an hour with that aren't involved with life or death. How do you do a show about an accountant or a steelworker week in and week out?" Fred Silverman, when asked why the close friends in series such as *Starsky and Hutch* always seemed to be policemen or doctors, exclaimed, "What are they going to be? Architects? What will happen to them?" The same network's research chief, Marvin Mord, observed that "once you have a character the audience cares about, and once you place that character in a life-jeopardizing situation, the audience is involved." And real situations? "You wouldn't watch it. People are not

willing to accept real problems in television drama. A program that attempts to deal with the harsh realities of life tends to turn viewers off."

This attitude is by no means confined to any one network. Perry Lafferty, for many years a top CBS programmer, once observed that he and his fellow programmers "couldn't think of a continuing hour show in which the hero didn't have the power of life and death—you have to give him a gun or a scalpel or a lawbook, and a jeopardy situation."

To one practitioner, that "jeopardy" is a matter of strict form. Quinn Martin, who produced *The Untouchables* and who heads the company that produces *The Streets of San Francisco, Cannon, Barnaby Jones, Most Wanted*, and other melodramas, explains: "It's a classic

A genuine break with dramatic formulas came with *The Waltons*. The large clan struggled through the Depression but never abandoned its familial ties. The family included Michael Learned as the mother (bottom left) and Will Geer as Grandpa (at the head of the table). At his right sits Richard Thomas as John-Boy; at his left is Ellen Corby as Grandma.

form: opening action, the middle jeopardy, and end action. You *need* the middle jeopardy to get the audience back after the minute-forty-five [commercial break]. If you don't have jeopardy in the middle break, they'll switch the channel. You have to have something so they'll say, 'Jesus, I want to see what's going to happen.' " (In soap opera, this heightened tension before the commercial is known as "the consternation fade-out.")

Third, jeopardy often implies some connection with violence, or, as networks prefer to describe it, "action-adventure." This issue has obsessed students of television since its inception. By 1950, studies were already underway on the effect of televised violence on children, and the U.S. Surgeon General's report of 1972 did find what it described as a "modest" causal link between televised violence and aggressive patterns of behavior. But, in fact, except for some notorious examples—*The Untouchables*, whose treatment of organized crime in the 1920s is surely the most violent television series in history, and a *Bus Stop* episode, "Told by an Idiot," featuring singer Fabian as a sadistic killer—the issue is not really violence at all. The essential element is a situation sufficiently tense and anxious to put the series' principal character in an atmosphere of danger, sufficiently simplistic to be resolved in fifty-two minutes. In the spring of 1975, the three networks, acting in what was later found to be unconstitutional collusion with the FCC, promulgated a "family hour." They moved sex and violence out of the early prime-time

Ralph Bellamy played Mike Barnett in *The Man Against Crime (above)*, one of the first (1949) action dramas; it was telecast live from the CBS Grand Central Station studios.

Richard Carlson played Herbert Philbrick, counterspy against domestic Communism in the Cold War action drama, *I Led Three Lives (top, left)*.

One of the most popular syndicated shows (distributed not by a network, but by ZIV, an independent production company) starred Broderick Crawford (left) in *Highway Patrol (bottom, left)*. This show, which began in 1956, concerned crime fighting but preached traffic safety as well, and made the police radio code "ten-four" a national catchphrase.

Jack Webb (left) was creator and star of *Dragnet (below)*, one of the first and best police-action shows. As Det. Sgt. Friday of the Los Angeles Police Department, Webb played a taut, clipped, policeman who wanted "just the facts, ma'am." Ben Alexander played his partner, Officer Smith. *Dragnet* was noteworthy for the character vignettes inserted between the action and for its compelling, memorable musical theme.

If drama involves in part the willing suspension of disbelief, then *Mission: Impossible,* a CBS hit series produced by Bruce Geller, set all kinds of dramatic records. *(Above):* Steven Hill (second from right) starred as the head of a remarkably talented team of spies (from left, Greg Morris, Barbara Bain, Martin Landau, and Peter Lupus) who weekly penetrated the security strongholds of sinister dictatorships by speaking heavily accented English and wearing uniforms. They never simply killed off their enemies; instead, they staged mock nuclear attacks and other electronic diversions to defeat evil. *(Right):* Peter Graves later assumed the role of chief commando.

Mannix was a typical detective show, starring Mike Connors as a private eye, Gail Fisher as his secretary, and a patterned sport jacket playing itself. Car chases, gun duels, life-and-death jeopardy every week...

One of the longest-running cop shows is CBS's *Hawaii Five-O,* starring Jack Lord. Although the show's scenery is its chief distinguishing characteristic, in 1977, after nine years, it was still on the air.

Robert Blake is the special asset of *Barretta,* an ABC detective show. He turns in what may well be the best acting on any regular series as the lead; in Blake's hands, the conventional cop-who-breaks-the-rules-but-gets-the-villain-and-cares-about-people format is credible.

period and generally toned down killings. What happened was that the shows featured violent treatment of *objects* instead of people. The "main titles" (the opening credits) of *Starsky and Hutch,* the biggest new "action" hit of the first Family Hour season, featured the classic car-chase screeching-tires montage with the two heroes running down villains, pursuing their foe—and concluding with a huge automobile explosion. Whatever can keep the audience concerned with the plight of the hero or heroine will suffice.

To many of the most successful members of the television industry, the all-but-exclusive franchise of the series in regularly scheduled television drama was

what one could expect of a mass medium. Frank Price, president of Universal Television, the biggest supplier of prime-time network programming for many years, notes that "in essence, TV has replaced the *Saturday Evening Post,* the slicks, hard-covered books, and radio. We have taken commercial fiction over." Universal, to be sure, has had its share of casualties in this world of rigid commercial-fiction rules. In one season, it supplied two series that attempted to bend these rules—*Sunshine,* about a young widower of the sixties generation and his daughter, and *The Law,* a worm's-eye view of the criminal justice system. Both survived only a short time on NBC.

The only recent successful anthology drama, NBC's *Police Story,* offers unusually realistic portrayals of the tensions and complexities in the lives of police officers. Here, Don Meredith (right) and David Groh (better known as Rhoda Morgenstern's ex-husband) appear in a 1976 episode.

What concerns others, including Frank Price and other successful people in the television industry, is that the rigid forms of these series never permit anything to happen to a character that might remotely be connected with reality. Almost fifteen years ago, Paul Monash, who developed *Peyton Place* for television as an early "nighttime soap opera," said of the series form that "your hero is a repetitious man who does not develop, in terms of himself, over the course of thirty hours a year." (As the cost of television shows increased, networks gradually reduced the number of original episodes from thirty-nine to twenty-two per season, beginning reruns in March.) *Police Story* executive pro-

ducer Stanley Kallis made the same point more than a decade later. A dramatic lead, he said, "is a function, not a human being. He's not gonna die, he's not gonna quit his job, he's not gonna grow in dimension. So the writer starts off with a leading character who's not interesting. You have to find meaningful problems for him to deal with. So each week, you give him a surrogate problem."

This kind of show, however well done it may be, however entertaining it may be—and some of them, such as *Kojak, N.Y.P.D.*, the early *Dragnet*, contained first-rate writing and acting—violates one of the essential precepts of drama: that the protagonist goes through a crisis from which he emerges changed. The essence of the series is that there be no *real* threat. Audiences, some television executives argue, don't *want* ambiguity. "Defeat and dreariness are what happens to you during the day," says ABC vice-president, Bob Shanks, in his book *The Cool Fire*. "At night, in front of the box, most people want to share in victories, associate with winners, be transported from reality." Every regular television watcher, including reasonably bright four-year-old children, knows that the protagonist will come out of every scrape in more or less the same shape he went into it, if for no other reason than because if Kojak gets shot, there's no more series.

Two of the best regular series to appear on network television were *The Defenders*, starring E. G. Marshall, and *East Side/West Side*, starring George C. Scott. Both shows had dared to go beyond the formula, not just by dealing with such controversial issues as abortion, capital punishment, residential integration, and even blacklisting, but by suggesting that not every dilemma ended happily. In the early 1960s, Marshall and Scott discussed whether their characters could develop over a period of time. Scott suggested that "if the classic idea of resolution is the goal, then at the end of some forecasted period, there should be some true resolution of the central character. There can be change in this sense. Some day, Brock [the social worker played by Scott] will face this—death, total resignation, incapacity . . . but not every week . . . We are really talking about the longest drama in history."

Indeed, in the last show of the series, Brock was given the opportunity to become a top aide to a charismatic political figure whose goal was the presidency of the United States. By implication, the end of the show was itself strong evidence that he did in fact take the job.

This premise, however, was anathema to the very idea of the continuing series and unthinkable in view of the commercial possibilities of a long-running dramatic show. By the 1960s, the networks had adopted a pattern called "deficit financing" of series. Put bluntly, this meant that the license fees paid to suppliers of shows (the money paid by a network for the right to run a show) did not pay the costs of producing that show. A series that ran for one or two years and was then canceled actually ended up costing the production company a fortune. The road to profit lay in keeping a show on the network long enough to accumulate a package of shows which could then be sold to independent stations and foreign markets for enormous profits. The concept of a continuing story was all but inconceivable to networks, apart from the daytime soap-opera form. In fact, when in the early 1960s Paul Monash suggested a "novelistic" show, taking the characters of Irwin Shaw's *The Young Lions* and following them through the

George C. Scott played social worker Neil Brock in *East Side/West Side,* a Talent Associates drama that many consider one of the finest regular series ever shown on commercial television. Here were poverty, unhappy endings, frustration—small triumphs and losses instead of the routine, ultimately trivial victories of the good guys on an assembly-line basis.

◄ Lee J. Cobb and Mildred Dunnock starred in Arthur Miller's
Death of a Salesman, shown on CBS in 1966. This study of an
ordinary man's tragedy, with its focus on character, was
uniquely suited to the television screen; it was a reminder of
what television had left behind.

In *Missiles of October,* an example of the "docu-drama"—the fictional portrayal of a real
event—Nehemiah Persoff and Howard DaSilva as Soviet leaders Andrei Gromyko and Nikita
Khrushchev *(left)* confront William Devane as President John Kennedy (shown here with James
Callahan as Kennedy aide Dave Powers) over the Cuban missile crisis.

CBS broadcast *Fear on Trial* in 1975, a fictionalized version of John Henry Faulk's attempt to fight the political
blacklist of the 1950s—in this case, a blacklist whose collaborators had included CBS. George C. Scott (left)
played defense attorney Louis Nizer, and William Devane (front, center) played Faulk.

One of the most popular movies of all time, *Gone with the* ▶
Wind, drew one of the largest audiences in television
history when it was broadcast in two parts on NBC in the
fall of 1976.

Dennis Weaver played a Taos, New Mexico, law enforcement
officer who brought his rural ways to New York in *McCloud.* This
drama, from ninety minutes to two hours long, is one of the
rotating series with the overall title *The NBC Sunday Mystery
Movie.*

An ABC made-for-TV movie that was at sharp variance with the
Indian stereotypes of early television westerns was *I Will Fight
No More, Forever,* which was broadcast in April, 1975. Here,
Ned Romero as Chief Joseph and Linda Redfern as his wife are
shown.

The made-for-TV movie frequently deals with themes considered too sensational or explicit for
regular series fare. NBC's *A Case of Rape (right)* starred Elizabeth Montgomery as the victim of
both a rapist and official callousness. CBS's *Helter Skelter,* a two-part dramatization of the story of
the Tate-LaBianca murders by the Charles Manson clan, was a ratings smash.

Cicely Tyson won critical acclaim and a large audience with her portrayal of a 110-year-old ex-slave in a 1974 CBS special, *The Autobiography of Miss Jane Pittman*. Here she challenges racial segregation by drinking at a "white-only" water fountain.

The long-running saga of the Bellamy family ▶ and their loyal core of servants, *Upstairs Downstairs*, originally shown on British television, won a devoted American following, especially among people who would never admit to enjoying soap opera. The Bellamy family ("Upstairs"; *top*) included (from left) Lesley-Anne Down, David Langton, and Simon Williams, served by Gordon Jackson. The servants ("Downstairs") were played by (from left) Angela Baddeley, Christopher Beeny, Gordon Jackson, Jacqueline Tong, and Jenny Tomasin. Jean Marsh (not shown), who played Rose, was one of the program's creators.

post–World War II years, programmers thought he was talking about a typical series such as *Combat* or *The Gallant Men*.

Instead, the network alternatives to the dramatic series, apart from the increasingly rare special offerings of *The Hallmark Hall of Fame*, and the short-lived *ABC Stage '67* and *CBS Playhouse*, were made-for-TV movies and the "long-form" (more than one-hour long) shows. The movies, pioneered by the perennially series-short ABC, did provide alternatives to the limited categories of dramatic series. Characters *could* pass through crises, even die, as did the star of the Chicago Bears, Brian Piccolo, in the story of his battle with cancer, *Brian's Song*. Delicate themes could be dealt with, including homosexuality, as in *That Certain Summer*. In the early 1970s, the networks began to present fictional portrayals of real-life events. These so-called "docu-dramas" explored, among other things, the Pueblo incident, the Cuban missile crisis, even—in *Fear on Trial*—television blacklisting of the 1950s.

NBC had begun programming long-form shows, first with *The Virginian*, and then with a number of ninety-minute- or two-hour-long shows with revolving characters, including *The Bold Ones* and *NBC Mystery Movie*. These helped relieve the more confining limits of the regular series. In essence, however, these two alter-

natives were minor bends in a narrow stream of programming possibilities. The made-for-TV movies, for example, often exploited genres that rarely survived in a regular series, such as fantasy and horror.

By the early 1970s, as Mercury Theatre veteran John Houseman wrote, original television drama was virtually a thing of the past on commercial television. More than half of the original network dramas were presented on public television, and half of those were imported from British television. Network drama was the province of artificial heroes struggling against artificial dilemmas, of no real relevance to the viewers, and always conquering them. Most of these heroes were without family, children, communities, distant from friends, neighbors, roots.

Ironically, it was one of those British imports that provided the first step toward what was to become a potentially significant alternative to the weekly, repetitive series. In 1969–1970, the Public Broadcasting System presented *The Forsyte Saga*—an adaptation of John Galsworthy's novels—in which characters grew, changed, even died. The response of the television industry was at first skeptical. Said David Victor, creator and executive producer of the *Marcus Welby, M.D.* series, "there was no follow-up for the next season. The secret of a good series is that you must be able to see

Peter Strauss and Susan Blakeley were two of the lead characters in the ABC "mini-series" adapted from Irwin Shaw's novel about two brothers in postwar America, *Rich Man, Poor Man*. The 1976 mini-series killed off one brother, Tom Jordache; the less successful weekly series the following year (*Rich Man, Poor Man—Book II*) ended by killing off Strauss's character, Rudy Jordache. The willingness to dispose of popular characters was a sharp break with conventional television tradition. Oh yes, Blakeley's character was killed off early in *Book II*.

episode thirty-five or forty-nine before you begin." But the reception to *The Forsyte Saga*, and, later, to London Weekend Television's *Upstairs Downstairs*, did trigger the interest of the commercial networks.

In 1975, CBS attempted to emulate the success of *Upstairs Downstairs* with its American version, *Beacon Hill*. Set in Boston of the post–World War I era, the story of the wealthy Lassiter family failed in the ratings. But the following spring, ABC scored a huge ratings hit with a "novel for television," a twelve-hour version of Irwin Shaw's *Rich Man, Poor Man*. Granted, the "mini-series," as it was known, had more than its share of commercial attractions, including a generous dose of sex and violence. But it also featured a continuing story in which the principal characters exhibited both positive and negative qualities. In the last episode of the presentation, one of the two leading characters was killed. If it was something less than high art, it was something more than the cookie-cutter that network drama had become.

The most popular show in American television history, ABC's *Roots*, was telecast in January, 1977, on eight consecutive nights. The twelve-hour version of author Alex Haley's search for his family's African origins and slave past—a blend of fact and fiction—captured more than half of the American population at some point in its run. Here Cicely Tyson as Binta admires the newborn Kunta Kinte, who will be sold into slavery as a young man. Maya Angelou looks on.

"The most trusted man in America," according to political polls, is Walter Cronkite, anchorman of *The CBS Evening News* since 1962.

The first major news event to transfix the American ▶
viewer was the congressional investigation into
organized crime chaired by Senator Estes
Kefauver (second from left), and spearheaded
by committee counsel Rudolph Halley (reading).
The hearings made Kefauver into a presidential
contender and helped Halley to become president
of the New York City Council.

NEWS AND SPORTS

The relentless demand of television for the biggest possible audience has reshaped the medium. In the process it has reinforced some of radio's forms, dismantled the early dramatic possibilities of the medium, and honed in on the development of appealing characters, personalities, people to draw the audience to the show. In two areas of television coverage, however, the event itself was so much the center of attraction that the exploitation of the personal was, for many years, relatively rare. These two areas—news and sports—seemed to contain such inherent dramatic properties that they attracted audiences not for whom they featured, but primarily for *what* they featured: linking the Atlantic and Pacific oceans instantaneously; bringing the World Series to the half of the nation that had never seen a major league baseball game (until 1955, no major league franchise was located west of the Mississippi except for St. Louis); taking the viewers inside a Senate hearing in a Manhattan office building to watch the hands of a camera-shy witness toy with a pair of glasses; giving a closer view of the field of action than a seat on the fifty-yard line could give.

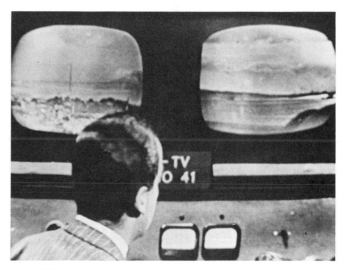

In November, 1951, Edward R. Murrow began a new television program, *See It Now*, by using the new coast-to-coast coaxial cable to telecast pictures of the Brooklyn Bridge and the Golden Gate Bridge at the same time to the same audience. "We are impressed," Murrow said.

91

An early example of a political use of broadcasting: ex-New York Governor Al Smith sings and dances at a 1935 Elks Minstrel Show while New York Mayor Fiorello LaGuardia joins in.

In both arenas, however, the medium began to overwhelm the event, with consequences that would ultimately reshape the events themselves. Television was able to change American preferences for sports even as it changed the texture of established sports—and eventually the traditional conception of what a sports event was. In the far more significant and sensitive field of news, television altered its own idea of what it could best accomplish, changing from a window on the world or a mirror of the world to a prism whose effects are still being debated. And, by realizing that those who reported the news were becoming as important to the audience as the news itself, television began to alter its approach to the news. By the middle of the 1970s, a revolution had taken place at the local news level that was forcing the network news divisions to ask what "news" really means.

News and sports were prominent in the earliest days of broadcasting. One of the first attempts to reach a wide audience was the radio broadcast on election night, 1920, by Pittsburgh's KDKA. When AT&T was establishing, and enforcing, its own monopoly on long-distance lines, it broadcast a 1922 football game from Chicago back to New York, and did the same with the Harvard-Yale football game of that year. The radio promised to bring people, separated by time and space from momentous events, as close to those events as the human voice could reach. Sports commentators—men like Bill Stern, Ted Husing, Graham McNamee—provided emotional, visual portrayals of boxing matches, World Series baseball games, and major college football games. On occasion, they all described the action not wisely, but too well; Bill Stern sometimes identified the wrong man carrying the ball for a touchdown, and then inserted an exciting, but nonexistent lateral pass to account for the difference. Other sports announcers "re-created" distant sports events by taking wire service accounts of the games and dramatizing them into a microphone, aided by special effects and prerecorded cheers.

Both the European war clouds and commercial competitive pressures helped to raise the stature of broadcast journalism in the late 1930s. CBS could not match the entertainment programming of the older and stronger NBC; it had, therefore, less to lose by clearing more time for news. In 1937, Edward R. Murrow was sent to London to begin building a European reporting team for CBS. A year later, the network inaugurated a "World News Roundup," featuring wireless reporting from around the world, with a team of reporters including Murrow, H. V. Kaltenborn, Eric Sevareid, William L. Shirer, Elmer Davis, and other journalistic giants.

So it was expected that television would emulate its big brother and make a major effort in these two fields.

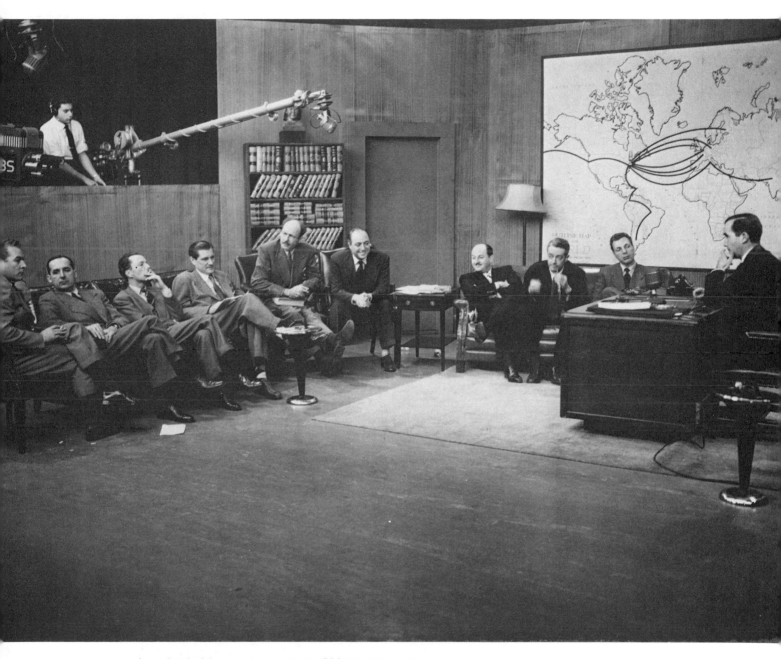

An early television appearance by the CBS "World News Roundup" team in 1955. Edward R. Murrow, moderating from the desk at far right, talks with (from left) Charles Collingwood, Ned Calmer, Winston Burdett, Eric Sevareid, Bill Costello, Larry Lesueur, David Schoenbrun, Howard K. Smith, and Richard C. Hottelet.

This May, 1939, Columbia-Princeton baseball game (*right*) was the first ever televised. That same year, this Fordham-Waynesburg football game (*below*) was shown on television. Note the camera mounted on a moving cart, to follow the line of scrimmage.

But here again, in the early days of television, technology limited what could be done. In the field of sports, at first only one, and then three cameras could be used to cover events live. From the initial faltering attempts—coverage of a Princeton-Columbia baseball game in May, 1939, two-camera coverage of a Dodgers-Reds game from Ebbets Field that same year, regular coverage of the World Series in 1947—it seemed clear that a sport scattered over the playing field such as baseball or football would be difficult to capture on the small screen. People would watch it, of course, because it was still closer to "the real thing" than radio. But television did best in those days, as it did in drama, where the action was on a smaller scale. The enormous interest in wrestling, boxing, and the roller derby in the first days of television was in large measure a product of the union between what was being seen and the limits of the television camera. These limits made it impossible for television to do more than point a camera at what was happening and let a radio-trained announcer fill in the words.

This picture from the broadcasting booth of a Giants-Dodger baseball game in 1947 illustrates a pervasive problem of baseball telecasting. The field is so wide and the players so dispersed that a television angle must be chosen to show either a close-up of the action or the flow of play.

An early television favorite still found on local stations was roller derby. It had the advantage of providing plenty of close-up violence for the visually hungry home viewer.

The first two network television anchors: CBS's Douglas Edwards *(top),* here shown in his 1948 debut, remained until 1962 when he was replaced by Walter Cronkite. On NBC, John Cameron Swayze *(above)* anchored the *Camel News Caravan* until Chet Huntley and David Brinkley succeeded him in the fall of 1956.

In the field of news, these limits also put stringent barriers on television's ambitions. Both CBS and NBC inaugurated a nightly news program almost as soon as they began regular programming. In 1948, NBC introduced a news show later called *Camel News Caravan,* with John Cameron Swayze's cordial "Ladies and gentlemen, and a good evening to you," opening the show; that same year, CBS started *Douglas Edwards with the News.* These shows, however, were essentially glorified radio programs. The networks had few film crews; most of the film had to be purchased from independent newsreel companies. There were many stories for which there was no film as it took time for film to be shipped back to the United States from abroad. So Edwards would display still photographs gathered through a wire service, while Swayze would "hopscotch the world for headlines," meaning that he would tell the viewers what was happening since he could not show them. What television could present, however, was the event itself. The Kefauver crime hearings of 1951 showed Frank Costello—but only his hands and eyeglasses, since he refused to allow his face to be photographed. It was riveting television. In 1952, the national conventions were televised for the first time, and terms such as "caucus" became widely shared jokes. The Army-McCarthy hearings in 1954 provided live, unrehearsed daytime drama for weeks on end, with a climactic denunciation of Joseph McCarthy by Joseph Welch (the courtly lawyer for the army), which helped end McCarthy's national popularity.

Networks were still experimenting with the best method of making news presentations visually arresting: NBC's *Victory at Sea,* a documentary series about World War II, went for the grandiose, with a stirring musical score by Richard Rodgers and a dramatic narrative accompaniment. CBS's *See It Now,* with Ed Murrow, went for the sparse: Murrow in a control room, with script plainly visible, reading large chunks of material, then cutting to film to make a clear point with an editorial message. He went after controversial issues: an air force officer who was denied his commission because of unspecified "questionable" political activities engaged in by his father and sister; a battle in Indianapolis between the American Legion and the American Civil Liberties Union; the work and tactics of Senator McCarthy. CBS's Walter Cronkite, a second-string correspondent in the earliest days of television, was pressed into service as host of one of the earlier efforts to combine documentary and fiction, *You Are There.* Major historical events were covered as if television were present. "Oh—oh, I see Caesar about to enter the Senate. Mr. Caesar, I wonder if we could get a word—"

Even in these first days of television news, there were

Meet two-thirds of the first group to be broadcast in compatible color, in 1953, on NBC. Kukla and Fran Allison are here; Oliver J. Dragon is otherwise occupied.

First shown on CBS in early 1971 after ABC rejected the Norman Lear pilot, the excellence of *All in the Family*'s cast (from right, Jean Stapleton, Carroll O'Connor, Sally Struthers, and Rob Reiner) and its unusual frankness in political and sexual matters made it the country's most popular show.

The Mary Tyler Moore Show, which debuted in 1970, was an uncommonly funny and sensitive portrayal of a modern career woman and her worker-friends. It retired as an undefeated champion in 1977, but it spawned two shows. Rhoda Morgenstern (*top;* with Ted Baxter, played by Ted Knight, and Mary Tyler Moore) went off to New York and an uncertain future in *Rhoda.* Valerie Harper's characterization of a smart, attractive, neurotic Jewish girl was fine, but the show floundered trying to balance Rhoda's independence against her marriage. Cloris Leachman (*bottom*) as *Phyllis,* whose show began in 1975, faced a different problem: how do you make a character who was essentially unpleasant appealing as a lead? Making her a widow was not enough; the show was canceled after two seasons.

The Bob Newhart Show (he's shown here with Marcia Wallace portraying girl-Friday Carol), produced and written by the same company that did *The Mary Tyler Moore Show*, MTM Productions, had an ambience similar to *The Mary Tyler Moore Show*. More important, it had *MTM* as a lead-in, as CBS sought to preserve the all-important "audience flow."

The made-for-TV movie, such as NBC's *Sybil* (starring Sally Field and Joanne Woodward), helped prove that television audiences would tolerate "long-form" dramas, ninety minutes or two hours in length, provided the story lines and characters were strong enough.

The return of show business glitter to variety shows was nowhere better illustrated than in this Cher special (*left*) in 1975, starring Bette Midler, Elton John, and Flip Wilson. The lavish costumes, sets, and imaginative use of color signified a return to the original concept of television variety—visual dazzle.

The more television broadcast parades, the more parades reshaped themselves to television's taste—with prerecorded production numbers and increasingly colorful and elaborate floats. The New York Thanksgiving Day parade (*right*), sponsored by Macy's, came to be primarily a TV attraction.

Four long-distance runners (*far right*): Bob Hope, Bing Crosby, John Wayne, and Frank Sinatra star in this 1975 comedy special.

From instant to permanent fame: Phyllis George, crowned Miss America in 1971 by the immortal Bert Parks, joined CBS to become the first successful female network sports announcer.

Search for Tomorrow has been on CBS since 1951. Here, Ann Williams and Val Dufour portray Eunice and John Wyatt. Eunice married John, her boss, following her first husband's death after a series of disasters.

Password, which debuted in 1961, was an innovative game show because it teamed an "ordinary" person with a well-known celebrity. Pictured here are host Allen Ludden and guest Peter Lawford playing the word-association game.

M*A*S*H—which became the most honest and outspoken of all situation comedies—survived frequent changes in time periods and cast members. In this picture, Loretta Swit and Alan Alda (next to her) remain from the original cast. Colonel Potter (Harry Morgan, seated at desk) took command from Colonel Henry Blake, and Captain B. J. Hunnicutt (Mike Farrell, third from right) replaced Trapper. Also shown is Father Mulcahy (William Christopher).

Burt Ward and Adam West starred as the classic comic book crime-fighting duo on *Batman*. The ABC television show of the mid-1960s, presented in high-camp style (with cartoon devices sprinkled into the show), was a short-lived, highly rated fad.

Since 1955, Bob Keeshan (center) has played Captain Kangaroo on this Monday-to-Friday CBS morning show: the *only* such regularly scheduled children's show on any of the three networks.

◀ The opening ceremony of the 1976 Winter Olympics at Innsbruck. ABC emphasized the color, pageantry, and the personalities of the athletes more than ever before.

To draw national attention to issues—and politicians—Senate hearings are frequently shown on daytime television. This picture is from the 1957 inquiry into criminal conduct in labor unions. Chief counsel to Senator John McClellan's committee was Robert Kennedy (fifth from left at committee table); to his left is Senator John Kennedy.

NBC's *Victory at Sea* was an early successful documentary, although it was enhanced by such dramatic effects as a Richard Rodgers score. Here American troops land at Utah Beach near France's Cherbourg Peninsula.

Ed Murrow *(opposite page)*, who acquired fame reporting from London on CBS radio, was host and cocreator of *See It Now*. His most famous show was his critical look at the tactics of Senator Joseph McCarthy in 1954. McCarthy replied on television *(above)*, calling Murrow "a leader of the jackal pack."

signs of what was to become a major trend. In 1953, Ed Murrow was nationally known by face as well as by voice. After risking his life on the rooftops during the bombing raids on London in World War II, he became a symbol of the knowledgeable, concerned correspondent. And, while he professed nervousness with television, he was suited to it, with a penetrating stare and a strong, angular face. That year, 1953, Murrow began hosting a second show, *Person to Person*. Here Murrow the newsman was replaced by Murrow the TV host. Television cameras roamed through the homes of the famous, guided by their occupants, as Murrow, from the homelike studio set, asked questions. Was it news as Murrow asked the Duchess of Windsor to play jacks, or Liberace to play a tune? Murrow said he hated the show, but it was his ticket to keep the probing *See It Now* series on the air. "To do the show I want to do," he said once, "I have to do the show that I don't want to do." The more interesting point, however, was that even in television's early days, and even with the man who stood for news integrity, there was pressure to make of this news symbol something else: a less "formidable," more easygoing, more comfortable kind of personality who would be welcome in the living rooms of celebrities. It was the glimmer of a tendency that was to grow.

Television news saw a different kind of emphasis on personality in 1956 at the national conventions. As with many experiences, particularly the vicarious kind, the first time it gave a dizzying series of sensations; the next time it began to pall. Television journalists had been enthralled just being there in 1952, watching politics, the demonstrations, the floor fights. But by 1956, it was a show they'd seen once before, and a show with a lot of dead space. At NBC, Chet Huntley and David Brinkley were given the job of anchoring the conventions, and during the lulls—of which there were many—the two began commenting lightheartedly on the convention hoopla. Brinkley talked about the occupations of the delegates, the absurd costumes, and some of the more outlandish resolutions and policies circulating. He spoke with an unusual vocal pattern, hitting some words hard to emphasize the silliness of what he was reporting, in a manner that forever earned him the adjective "wry." The team was so successful that they replaced John Cameron Swayze on the NBC news show in the fall of 1956.

But what had made them successful as a team? More or better news? Or something else? Dick Wald, currently president of NBC News, says that "after years of solemn reporters, here were two human beings who actually talked to each other." There was an appealing personality mix between the serious Huntley and the less inhibited Brinkley. By now, television had discovered that however much the news operation wanted to

(opposite): Ed Murrow was the genial host of the highly rated *Person to Person,* which featured elaborately informal chats with celebrities. The Duke and Duchess of Windsor *(top;* she's playing jacks), and Elizabeth Taylor and Mike Todd *(center)* were among the guests.
(opposite, below): The Kennedy presidency relied heavily on television to reinforce the image of glamour and elegance. In 1962, Jacqueline Kennedy took the American people on a tour of the White House.

Chet Huntley and David Brinkley were first teamed by NBC at the 1956 Democratic National Convention in Chicago. The combination of the somber Huntley and the witty Brinkley made them a highly successful anchor team when they replaced John Cameron Swayze on the network's nightly news show in the fall of 1956. Brinkley again became coanchor of the NBC evening news show in 1976.

The presidential nominating conventions furnish a classic case of how television news moved from observer to active participant in the political process. The first conventions in which television was a full-fledged observer were those of 1952. Adlai Stevenson, as governor of Illinois, gave a witty, eloquent welcoming address at the Democratic convention *(top)* that made him nationally known instantly. With the active assistance of President Truman, Stevenson became the Democratic presidential nominee.

Politicians know that television takes the traditional "home and family" images and makes them exceptionally vivid. At the 1976 Democratic National Convention *(above)*, presidential nominee Jimmy Carter is surrounded by mother, daughter, sons, and wife.

These contrasting views of the 1976 Republican convention illustrate television's supremacy. From the delegate's view *(top)*, little is clear; from the perch of the anchor booth *(opposite page, top;* NBC's John Chancellor, left, and David Brinkley are shown here) the entire hall is visible, and information flowing in from all over the floor and the candidates' headquarters keeps the reporters up to date.

By 1968, television coverage of the Democratic convention *(opposite page, bottom)*—and of the disturbances in the streets outside Chicago's convention hall—had become a national issue, with charges of distortions and unfair emphasis on police brutality. Richard Nixon's renomination at the 1972 Republican convention *(above)* was almost totally staged for television; a prepared "script" even indicated when "spontaneous" demonstrations would erupt.

◀ Professional basketball, long a stepchild of major league sports, was one of many sports that received multi-million-dollar infusions from network television. In this Knicks-Celtics game of the early 1970s, Dave DeBusschere shoots against Steve Kuberski, while Jerry Lucas looks on.

Five hundred feet away from the action at Yankee Stadium, a bleacher fan *(left)* gets closer to home plate via portable television. From the broadcast booth at the stadium, Mel Allen served as "the voice of the Yankees" from 1939 until 1964. Like many other sports announcers, Allen developed his own signatures: "Going, going, *gone!*" to describe a home run and "How *about* that!" to describe an outstanding play.

remain separate from the entertainment aspect of television, there were fundamental reasons why such a separation could not fully succeed. In part, it was because audiences used television as an entertainment medium. They could, in a newspaper, easily distinguish between the serious news and the comics, but television news was something that happened a few moments each day (networks were only broadcasting fifteen minutes until 1963), in between the shows. In part, it was that *anyone* who was on television every night, coming into the home, promoted feelings of both awe and intimacy. He or she was someone the viewer knew, trusted, liked, believed. Viewers were not likely to pick and choose among competing news programs on the basis of who explained the federal budget better. Once viewers recognized a threshold level of respectability and competence among the

news shows—recognition that perennially eluded the younger, poorer, traditionless American Broadcasting Company—they would pick the people they most wanted in their homes. In the second half of the 1950s, that meant Huntley and Brinkley. And it also meant a growing realization among news executives that the bearer of the news was as important, if not more important, than the news itself.

In the field of sports as well, the late 1950s and early 1960s were significant, for sports executives discovered more about what the public wanted from a sports program—and why. In the 1950s, baseball was considered the national pastime. Football was then a sport best appreciated by collegians, and the pro game ran a poor second to baseball in its following. Basketball was a high school sport of fanatical followers, but pro ball had never built a league with staying power. And

◀ The packaging of sports and the networks' capacity to feed a seemingly insatiable appetite for more sports coverage led to the expansion of pregame and half-time shows. CBS developed *NFL Today* to provide pregame reports and features. Here, then–CBS Sports vice-president Robert Wussler chats with Phyllis George, the first successful woman sports commentator.

An early demonstration of television's up-close ability was provided in this 1947 football game between two New York professional football teams, the Brooklyn Dodgers and New York Yankees. Yankee coach Ray Flaherty watched the game on television from the sidelines, looking for missed assignments and hidden angles.

An early attempt to educate the sports viewer was in this 1950 telecast. A white arrow or "electronic pointer" was used to show who was carrying the ball. In later years, instant-replay devices provided half a dozen views of the same play, in slow motion.

hockey, in the late 1950s, was a league with six teams in only four American cities, whose following was loyal but small. But baseball was not a sport well suited to the world of television. Its field of action was wide, diffuse; its most exciting plays, such as the extra base hit with men on base, could only be covered by fragmenting the action or by pulling the camera back so far that the players appeared antlike. In addition, there were 154 games a year, and many baseball teams permitted coverage of every home game as well as out-of-town games. In New York, which had three baseball teams until 1958, more than 400 baseball games were broadcast to the same community each year—and that was overexposure with a vengeance. One of the first things

Dodgers owner Walter O'Malley did when he moved the team from Brooklyn to Los Angeles was to black out home games; whether as a consequence or not, the Dodgers have been among the most successful baseball franchises almost every year since.

Football, by contrast, was a weekend sport exclusively. It was played in the autumn and winter, when the weather was more likely to keep people indoors. Both the college and professional seasons included a dozen games or less, so every game was crucial. And, in a burst of shrewdness, the National Football League had negotiated an agreement with CBS that flatly prohibited the telecasting of any home games. The road games therefore stimulated the fan's interest, which could be

In 1969, the American Football League—which had been kept alive by a network television contract—proved itself equal to the older National Football League when the New York Jets upset the Baltimore Colts in the Super Bowl. Joe Namath, the swinging single Jet quarterback, became a six-figure spokesman for products long after his arm—and his team—stopped producing.

satisfied only by attending the home games in person. Further, in 1958, the New York media, deserted by the baseball Brooklyn Dodgers and New York Giants, who had both pulled up stakes for California, found in the New York Giants of the National Football League a new source of affection. The Giants returned the compliment by fighting the Baltimore Colts for the NFL championship in a sudden-death overtime game which many sports writers called "the greatest football game ever played." This hoopla fed the appetite of sports fans for professional football—a sport whose violent contact could be reached by the Zoomar lens, whose deceptive fakes, hand-offs, and quick cuts by running backs and pass catchers could be brought to the home

viewer in a manner inaccessible to the fan at the football stadium. From 1958 to 1969, the sport of professional football exploded. A newcomer, the American Football League, survived a dearth of spectators in the early sixties because of a $42 million, five-year contract it signed with NBC on the heels of the New York Jets' acquisition of Joe Namath. In the mid-1960s, CBS paid the National Football League $14 million a year for the rights to its games; in 1970, ABC bought the rights to *Monday Night Football* for almost $9 million a year.

College football, an exclusive province of ABC (save for the postseason bowl games), received a novel treatment under the direction of Roone Arledge, who was later to become president of ABC Sports. Rather

The 1976 Sugar Bowl—matching up Pittsburgh and Georgia—was one of many sports events shifted into prime-time schedules over the years to maximize television audiences. The Sugar Bowl is now played in the New Orleans Superdome, where the vagaries of weather are overcome, so that—among other things—the television picture remains clear.

Inevitably, those who reported the news on television became as recognizable, and as famous, as those whose activities they were reporting. Here, exchanging on-camera remarks during the 1968 Democratic convention (from right) are floor reporters Sander Vanocur, John Chancellor, Frank McGee, and Edwin Newman.

than emphasizing the complexity of the game, Arledge began to focus on the *pageantry:* the faces of the cheerleaders, the intensity of the crowd. Hand-held cameras recorded close-up reactions of players on the benches, of coaches and officials, of members of the band as their team went down to defeat. Under Arledge's guidance, the coverage of college football beginning in 1960 underwent a fundamental change which was to alter the premise of television coverage of all sports. Instead of bringing the home viewer to the game, television was taking the viewer into a game, as an event with intense emotional involvement — which no spectator at a game could ever grasp. It was to become a much more intimate glimpse of sports than the "real" event could provide. It was beyond reality.

By the early 1960s, the basic form of what is now known as the nightly network news had taken shape. NBC was

featuring Huntley and Brinkley, reporting from New York and Washington, D.C., respectively. In 1962, Walter Cronkite replaced Douglas Edwards as anchorman on the *CBS Evening News.* In 1963, Elmer Lower, hired away from NBC by ABC, began to make of that spit-and-baling-wire news operation a professional operation. That same year, both CBS and NBC news went to a half hour, with the tacit understanding that in most major markets the network news would be carried at the same time. (ABC did not expand its news to a half hour until 1967.) If either network had competed against news with an entertainment program, it would have wiped the news show off the ratings chart.

None of the networks could have put its news programs on the air, other than on the five stations around the country each of them owned and operated, through its own efforts. But, as Edward Epstein has documented in *News from Nowhere*, the Federal Communications

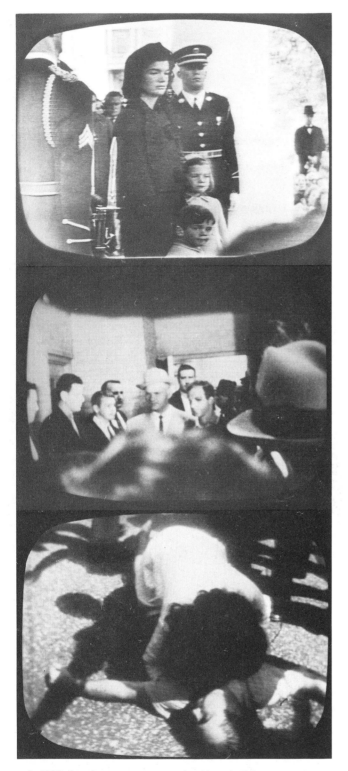

In 1963, Americans were mesmerized by television coverage after the assassination of President John Kennedy. The solemnity of the funeral *(top)* and the shocking murder of accused assassin Lee Harvey Oswald by Jack Ruby *(center)* were conveyed with a sense of immediacy and drama. Television also captured the shooting of Alabama Governor George Wallace *(bottom)* in the midst of his 1972 presidential campaign. Wallace's wife, Cornelia, comforts her wounded husband.

Commission in effect compels local network affiliates to carry network news by making national news coverage an important item in judging whether station licensees serve the public interest. And local stations simply find it cheaper to carry network news and documentary shows than to attempt to finance their own operations. Epstein quotes one NBC executive as acknowledging, "Without the FCC, we couldn't line up enough affiliates to make a news program or documentary worthwhile."

By the same token, the exploding profits in network television in the 1960s made the money-losing prime-time documentaries a less and less attractive commodity. Ed Murrow's *See It Now* had been eased out of the CBS prime-time schedule and consigned to the weekend "ghetto," to be replaced by the sometimes excellent, sometimes soft *CBS Reports*. (Murrow himself left the company with a good deal of bitterness in 1961 to become director of President John F. Kennedy's United States Information Agency.) This illustrates the double standard of the networks, which criticize their "money-hungry" affiliates while presenting a generally unbroken history of squeezing public affairs out of every conceivably profitable time slot.

However, changing conditions made the nightly news shows more financially attractive by the early sixties. The working population of America was coming home more and more by auto, less and less by mass transit, where the evening paper was a welcome companion. With a choice of three network news shows that were broadcast about the time working Americans got home, the demand for afternoon and evening papers was shrinking. No news in an evening paper could hope to compete in timeliness with network television news; and the launching of Telstar I in 1962, followed by other communications satellites, had made it possible to transmit news from anywhere in the world directly to a network broadcast center when events warranted. If anyone had any doubt about the power of television to communicate major events to the entire nation, it was dispelled forever during the four days from November 22 to November 25, 1963. Millions of Americans saw these scenes—the first bulletin that President Kennedy had been shot in Dallas, Walter Cronkite broadcasting directly from a CBS newsroom, the pomp of the funeral and the tributes, and, shockingly, the suspected assassin of John Kennedy, Lee Harvey Oswald, murdered on live television by Jack Ruby in the basement of the Dallas jail—as the country held vigil by its television sets.

Yet this very power was beginning to raise some bothersome questions. Take the simplest consideration—time. A thirty-minute newscast less commercials leaves twenty-two minutes to tell the American people of the important events that happened during the day. No one at the networks pretends that television news

Almost unimaginable to an earlier generation, live television coverage from the moon was seen by 750 million people all over the world in the summer of 1969; it was the most witnessed event in world history.

Man wasn't there, but TV was, telecasting back to Earth the first photos from the planet Mars in 1976.

The first American to orbit the Earth, John Glenn, became an instant celebrity after his 1962 Project Mercury flight. Twelve years later, he became a United States senator.

Senator Sam Ervin and chief counsel Sam Dash are shown at the 1973 Watergate hearings. To preserve their daytime profits, networks rotated coverage of the hearings, except when moments of high drama, such as the testimony of former presidential counsel John Dean, were expected. Public television provided daily coverage throughout. The hearings made a national catchphrase of Senator Howard Baker's question, "What did the president know, and when did he know it?"

Sometimes contentious, sometimes tendentious, David Susskind has been moderating a discussion show *(Open End,* later renamed *The David Susskind Show)* for almost twenty years. In this 1960 program, Susskind talks with members of the Soviet delegation to the United Nations.

The longest-running public affairs show on television is NBC's *Meet the Press*. Since 1947 public figures such as Ronald Reagan, shown here, have used this show as a forum to present their views

can be anything more than a headline service; in a famous experiment, CBS News executive Richard Salant printed the text of a typical nightly news show and it filled less than a full page of a metropolitan newspaper. Of course, this experiment proved little; after all, except for major metropolitan dailies, the typical newspaper does not have much after page one that is any more consequential than television entertainment. The more interesting question about time has to do with the nature of a television news program. As with its entertainment offerings, a network must seek to draw the largest possible audience with its news program. And, as *Time*'s Thomas Griffiths has noted, "a crucial difficulty is that, unlike print, where the eye can skip around, you cannot jump to the broadcaster's next item, so each item must interest everyone a little and dare not go on long." To watch a television news program, then, is to

be given a taste of information about a range of subjects in an order and package utterly controlled by the news show. Unlike a reader with a newspaper, a viewer is not in control of what he sees. He is instead at the mercy of a news show that cannot in any sense touch on regional, cultural, or neighborhood distinctions, but, rather, has to present the most general kinds of stories.

It is impossible to say whether significant numbers of Americans would have grown to resent the power of television news had American society continued to be a politically placid arena. But with the explosive 1960s, Americans began to confront some hard issues. The civil-rights movement—sit-ins, freedom rides, voter registration marches—was covered by a national news-gathering operation overwhelmingly sympathetic to black demands. But these reports were carried to some regions with a sizable portion of the populace who were

The extensive network news coverage of the civil-rights movement—including this 1957 struggle to integrate Little Rock, Arkansas, schools—convinced some Southerners that television networks were biased in their news coverage.

militantly against these demands. These viewers saw in network television not simply a recording of these events, but an advocacy of change. And such criticism was not confined to the South; as black demands grew, especially as they spread to the North, large numbers of citizens saw themselves in opposition to the protest movements being shown every night on the news. By 1964, their reaction could be seen in three Democratic presidential primaries *outside* the Deep South, as Alabama Governor George Wallace, then a strong segregationist, won 35 to 45 percent of the vote, making one of his major targets the national television networks.

This sense of resentment against the most visible and powerful of news organizations found fertile soil among other constituencies. The certainty among many that the entire national press corps was opposed to Barry Goldwater's candidacy for president in 1964—a certainty with a foundation in fact—produced in them a deep-seated resentment against the national press. And when the war in Vietnam began to escalate in 1965, it was the television networks, covering the war with few official restrictions, that brought to American

homes pictures of the face of war that had never been shown before: not friendly troops welcomed by the populace, but troops setting fire to villages with cigarette lighters; troops cutting off the ears of dead combat foes; allies spending American tax money for personal gain. There was no way to turn the page, no way to ignore the news that was posing such a challenge to traditional assumptions about American participation in foreign conflicts. There was no way to ignore what network television was showing America—about the cities, the campuses, the war—but that did not mean it had to be believed. This credibility gap—not between president and people, but between people and their primary source of information—created the opportunity for a national administration to make the network news a prime political target.

Richard Nixon's relationship with the press had never been warm; after his 1962 loss in the California gubernatorial election, he held his famous "last press conference" in which he pledged that the press wouldn't have Nixon to kick around anymore. (He also paid tribute to television news for keeping the written press honest.)

The issue of unfair TV coverage exploded during the war in Vietnam, when TV brought into American homes the ugly side of the war. Two of the most famous incidents televised were the burning of a Vietnam village by American troops (*top, left;* shown in an August, 1965, field report by CBS newsman Morley Safer) and the summary execution of a suspected Vietcong agent by South Vietnam's National Police Chief Nguyen Ngoc Loan *(left)* during the 1968 Tet offensive. Television was specifically accused of publicizing the growing demands of antiwar protesters *(above)* in the late 1960s.

When he and his aides took over the White House and a war in Vietnam they had not begun, they quickly made that war theirs, and saw in the broadcast press—"the media," they called it, instead of using the all-American word "press"—a committed opponent of the Nixon administration's policy. So White House speechwriter Pat Buchanan crafted a speech for Vice-President Spiro Agnew. Delivering it in Des Moines, Iowa, in November, 1969, Agnew attacked "a small group of men, numbering perhaps no more than a dozen anchormen, commentators, and executive producers, [who] settle upon the twenty minutes or so of film and commentary that's to reach the public" as "a tiny, enclosed fraternity of privileged men elected by no one and enjoying a monopoly sanctioned and licensed by government."

Several points need to be made. First, the Agnew attack—indeed, the overall White House offensive against the television network news departments—was explicitly political, based on the networks' practice of providing (in Agnew's words) "instant analysis and querulous criticism" instead of permitting Nixon to speak to the public without challenge. This was no principled assault upon concentration of media ownership, only upon those elements of concentrated power that provided opposing voices a chance to match the president's words. Second, the merits of the charge itself contained a substantial level of accuracy. In covering the 1968 Democratic convention, the networks *had* distorted reality by their timing in broadcasting the tapes of the police-youth confrontation in the streets of Chicago. There *were* only three national avenues by which to reach the public. And there was no real diversity in news presentation, no way to challenge Walter Cronkite's catchphrase that so irritated disaffected viewers and say to him, "No, that *isn't* the way it is, at least, not all of it."

And overarching all of these disputes was the undeniable fact that television news had become the focal point of the political process. This was symbolized by the presidential debates between Vice-President Richard Nixon and Senator John Kennedy in 1960. The same Richard Nixon who had helped trigger a political revolution in 1952 by sitting down and speaking directly

115

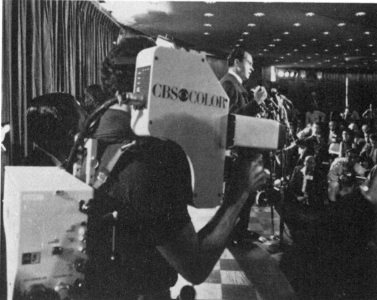

In an effort to smother the press with access and affection, President Johnson invited the wives and children of reporters to attend an outdoor press conference in May, 1964 *(above)*. It did not succeed in bridging the "credibility gap" that helped erode Johnson's political popularity. After the Watergate revelations, President Nixon's press conferences *(left)* turned into emotional wrestling matches with the press.

In his November, 1969, attack on the broadcast media—carried live by all three ▶ television networks—Vice-President Spiro Agnew signaled the start of the most intense confrontation between a national administration and the press. The speech was followed up by repeated attempts to bring network broadcasting more in line with the policies, especially the foreign policies, of the Nixon administration.

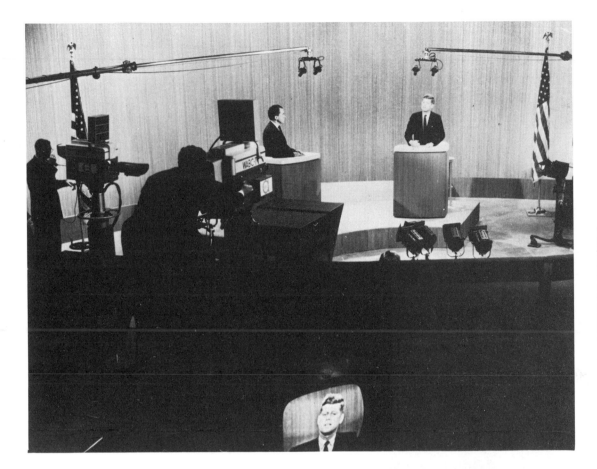

In 1960, John Kennedy met Richard Nixon *(top)* in the first televised debate between presidential candidates. The more relaxed, telegenic Kennedy won the image battle, whatever the substantive point scoring. Sixteen years later, Jimmy Carter and Gerald Ford *(bottom)* met in a series of debates. They were sponsored by the League of Women Voters in order to avoid the equal-time laws preventing network sponsorship of debates. Here, television dominated the words and body language of both contenders.

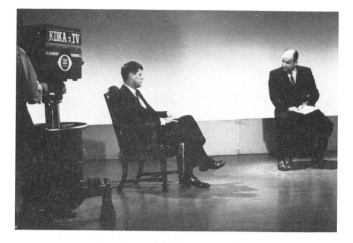

The 1960 campaign of John Kennedy was built on an understanding of television. Here, in 1959, Kennedy appears on a Pittsburgh public affairs show hosted by Paul Long with high school and college students—one of hundreds of local TV appearances the underdog senator made. Kennedy demonstrated television's power to bypass the traditional party structure and reach the voters directly in their homes.

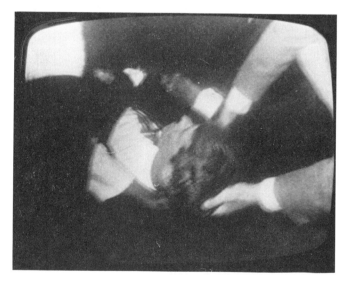

Television networks always had a camera crew near Senator Robert Kennedy in his 1968 presidential campaign; they anticipated an assassination attempt. When it came in June, 1968, in California, CBS's Jim Wilson was there to photograph the consequences.

to the American people—face to face—in his famous "Checkers" speech had forgotten this lesson in 1960. In that first debate, Vice-President Nixon had looked at John Kennedy, at the moderator, at the studio audience—everywhere except the one place that counted: directly into the camera. The success of John Kennedy, in using television to overcome his youth and in bringing the force of his personality directly into the American home, was a new political phenomenon. Politicians at every major level began to realize that access to television could replace the traditional methods of gaining political power. Either through free television time or through heavy political advertising or a combination of the two, a politician could overcome the disadvantages of obscurity or rejection by the party establishment. Moreover, the continuing revolution in technology enabled television to cover politicians not just in halls with lighting and electrical outlets, but in factories, in private homes, anywhere a politician might choose to go in order to obtain an effective visual backdrop. In 1972, Democratic nominee George McGovern structured his entire presidential campaign to appear in three different media markets in the same day. And candidates were concerned less with the traditional forms of campaigning and more with the way they would appear on the evening news. The device that had begun by pointing at the traditional political processes had reshaped the nature of what it had intended originally to observe.

An analogous revolution in sports was also taking place through the 1960s and early 1970s. Sports had become a big-time, multi-billion-dollar industry, and television began to exert its inexorable influence to build the biggest possible audiences. The most obvious indication is the shift toward nighttime sports, since there are millions more people who watch television at night than during the day. So by the mid-1970s, traditional daylight events—the World Series games in midweek, the All-Star games, at least one professional football game each week—were shifted into prime time to gain bigger audiences and increased advertising revenues. Of course, by the time the World Series was played, what with four major league baseball divisions, a longer season, and playoffs, it was mid-October when nights get cool. But television was no longer an interested observer; it was an equal, perhaps senior partner with the game itself, spending millions of dollars for the rights to the World Series alone. Sore muscles and an occasional missed grounder because of the cold could hardly offset the power of the dollar.

A more fundamental change in the nature of sports was triggered by ABC's Roone Arledge in 1961, when

ABC began broadcasting *Wide World of Sports*. At the time, the network had the rights to no major sports events save college football. It proceeded to create its own sports magazine, a two-hour show which broke with several existing conventions at the same time. Broadcast sports had always stressed its capacity to bring the viewer to an event as it was taking place; *Wide World of Sports* cut between live, taped, and filmed sports events, some of which had taken place days before in places around the world. Broadcasting had confined itself to traditional, major sports; *Wide World* covered everything from barrel jumping to stock car races to funny car auto-wreck championships—and drew large audiences as a result. The weekend sports audience, Arledge discovered, was interested in action, movement, spectacle. That it might be a sport viewers had never played, witnessed, or cared about before seemed not to matter. It was good television, and that was what counted.

The technological revolution had already shown audiences traditional games in totally untraditional ways. The isolated camera, the slow-motion instant replays, the pretaped interviews that were run as an athlete participated in an event had shattered the way the American viewer looked at sports. He was being bombarded with more visual data than a spectator at the game could see—resulting in the installation of huge television screens in some new sports arenas, affording the paying customer almost as good a view as the home viewer had. Further, the camera had brought the viewer far closer to an athlete than the paying customer, scrambling for an autograph after the game, could hope to reach. Before television, a sports event could only be witnessed as a spectacle—an event with competitors, *not* personalities. Television changed that, showing home viewers the faces behind the football helmets and close-ups of other athletes. Their private lives, contract battles, social and political views became as much grist for the gossip mills as had the lives of Hollywood stars a generation earlier.

In fact, so effective was television at turning athletes into celebrities that networks found they could create their own sports packages, which could outdraw traditional sporting events. In the early 1970s, CBS had professional basketball and NBC had major league hockey on Sundays. ABC created an artificial "Superstars" competition, with athletes competing in a kind of decathlon marathon, and drew the lion's share of the Sunday sports audience. By the mid-1970s, networks had begun to replace the existing sports structure with "Team Superstars," "Challenge of the Sexes," and a raft of other such events based on the premise that a viewer would watch a well-known personality in some form of competition regardless of the level of the game.

Sports goes showbiz—in 1973, ABC telecast this "Tennis Battle of the Sexes" between Bobby Riggs and Billie Jean King. Ms. King won in three straight sets. More significant was the ability of television to package its own sports event, irrespective of the intrinsic athletic competition.

Sports and celebrities—they go together. Here a scene from the Bob Hope Desert Classic, with the comedian himself and golfer Doug Sanders.

Mark Spitz won seven gold medals as a United States swimmer in the Olympics of 1972—he's shown here after helping to capture the 4 x 100 meter medley swim—but his attempt to parlay that triumph into a television career, as an actor and commercial spokesman, fizzled.

The mixture of sports and celebrities has become a more frequent offering of networks. Here Farrah Fawcett-Majors meets Bill Cosby in a 1977 CBS package called "Challenge of the Sexes," which includes battles between celebrities as well as athletes.

Whether it was Jimmy Connors battling Ilie Nastase or Farrah Fawcett-Majors battling Bill Cosby on the tennis courts, the audience wanted to see *stars*, and the dividing line between athletes and entertainers was all but eradicated. The trend toward booking celebrities reached some kind of high—or low—in 1977 when CBS broadcast "Evel Knievel's Death Defiers," featuring Evel Knievel attempting one of his motorcycle jumps. The show drew high ratings, even though Knievel had injured himself in a practice run. The network apparently felt this presentation had crossed the line, and canceled its option on a second show.

Televised sports began by showing viewers an event they would otherwise have missed; it began by observing a real-life contest between highly skilled competitors as it was occurring. Its technological genius enabled it to cover these events with a new eye—to place cameras at the Olympics in such a way that the brilliance of a skier or a gymnast or a runner could be brought closer to a viewer than ever before in history. It was possible to see Nadia Comaneci balancing in

Television was criticized for glorifying Evel Knievel, the daredevil motorcycle rider. Knievel is seen here leaping fourteen buses on an ABC appearance.

Muhammad Ali, then-unseated heavyweight champion thanks to a dispute with the government over draft resistance, plays with Howard Cosell's toupee in a 1972 appearance. Cosell, who defended Ali, gained a national reputation as a "controversial" sports announcer, who, in his own words, liked to "tell it like it is."

midair, to see her footwork, her facial expression, her body control all at once. Sports and television, in this sense, seemed made for each other.

But the appetite of the viewers for the personal glimpse had extended beyond reality. They demanded more than skill; they demanded charm, wit, eloquence, and controversy as well. When ABC televised the 1976 Olympics, the network showed not just what a runner could do, but where that runner came from, how he or she lived; it brought the viewers, in the words of the network, "up close and personal." The question remains whether this emphasis on who an athlete is rather than what he can do on the field is covering sports—or smothering it.

It was perhaps inevitable that sooner or later television would personalize not only those it covered but also the people doing the coverage. As television reporters discovered with the growth of television news, a face frequently on camera becomes as well known as that of any politician or "celebrity." Network regulars—Walter Cronkite, David Brinkley, Chet Huntley, John Chancellor, Harry Reasoner—found it increasingly difficult to cover a campaigning politician, since the crowds gathered not around the politician but around the reporters.

What was less inevitable was the deliberate attempt to attract viewers, specifically on the level of local television news, by emphasizing the personal attributes of reporters.

This trend had its unintended roots in an innovative news show on KQED, a northern California public television station. In the late 1960s, attempting to break with the rigid formula of local news, the station introduced *Newsroom*, a one-hour local show in which reporters sat around a horseshoe-shaped table and talked with each other about the stories they were covering. As the reporters combined their factual presentations with a more conversational approach to news, this enabled other reporters to bring up and clarify points that might be confusing to the viewer as well.

The *appearance* of this process, without much of the substance, materialized on local newscasts at the end of the 1960s, triggered principally by the *Eyewitness News* format of the ABC-owned and -operated stations. Here the news personnel were made the focus of the presentation. Instead of cutting from a news report to a commercial and then to the sportscaster, the anchorman exchanged "cross talk" with the weatherman ("Gave us a beautiful day yesterday, Pete, can you do it again today?") or sports reporter ("Hey, Biff, what's the matter with our Rams?"). On a lighter story, a reporter became *part* of it; for example, a reporter would end a story on a costume exhibition by donning a costume. A touch football game report would end with the reporter signing off, picking up the football, and throwing a pass. An anchorman also "quizzed" a reporter after a story, less to make substantive additions than to create the image of involvement ("Dan, do they know *why* the principal went berserk?" "Not yet, Bob").

These newscasts were structured around the premise that the television audience, whether for news or entertainment, was looking for the same values: action, pace, involvement, people to believe and care about. The promotional ads for New York's *Eyewitness News* showed the reporters and anchormen in each other's communities—attending a wedding or an ethnic festival, teasing each other, laughing with each other. The shows open with the news team walking—or jogging—onto the set, to create a sense of motion. Some local news shows, as if they were a situation comedy instead of a news program, began to deliberately develop on-camera character traits of reporters and news readers: a "feud" between anchorman and sportscaster, a flirtation between anchorman and entertainment critic.

The search for the winning news format was understandable; by the mid-1970s, local news was an enormously profitable venture, accounting for a third to a half of a local station's profits. Local newscasts were

In the early days of television, a woman's place on the news was confined to light features and an appearance as a "weathergirl." Shown is Jeanne Parr, a weathergirl on the *CBS Sunday News* in the early 1960s.

The local news team as "happy family" on one of the ABC-owned and -operated stations using an "Eyewitness News" formula, Los Angeles station KABC-TV. Shown from left are Jerry Dunphy, anchor, Eddie Alexander, Dr. George Fishbeck, weatherman and raconteur, and anchor Christine Lund.

routinely one-hour long in the bigger cities, with ninety minutes and even two hours a growing pattern in the biggest media markets. To the local news directors, under intense pressure to produce the highest ratings for the highest dollar—knowing that a single rating point could make a million-dollar difference in advertising revenues—it was crucial to develop winning news personalities and formats. Increasingly, they turned to news consultants (Frank Magid and McHugh and Hoffman, Inc. being the two most famous companies), who would study an operation and recommend specific changes, usually shorter stories, a greater number of stories, more use of action film, more warmth and friendliness on the set. Many local stations began to hire reporters with no journalistic experience, looking only for the charismatic face and voice that would pull the audience to their stations at six and eleven o'clock. This trend led CBS's Charles Kuralt to observe that his overriding impression of local newscasts was one of "hair." (One local station in Boston put a young newscaster through five different changes of hairstyle in a single year.)

More substantively, local television stations began to expand the definition of news by reaching into those areas developed by newspapers and magazines whose hard-news appeal had been lessened by television. Around the country, newspapers and magazines emphasized service features with articles on changing life-styles, how to cope in the modern world, where to find bargains, how to survive in a big city. Newspapers had for many years run "Action Line" columns, helping citizens fight their way through government or corporate bureaucracy. Television also made its news departments more feature-oriented, seeking to include the life of the *viewer*, and not just the life of the community, in its broadcasts. Consumer complaints, health tips, advice on bargain shopping, how to "beat the system"—the longer local news programs carried all of these features, and by doing so completed a curious circle. Television news had originally assumed that its strength lay in bringing the viewer to distant places and faraway events, in broadening his horizon. And, after thirty years, it found that a viewer could be reached most powerfully by talking to him about his personal,

In direct contrast to the informal news approach is *The MacNeil/Lehrer Report,* shown nightly on the Public Broadcasting System. Reporters Robert MacNeil and Jim Lehrer take one story, using experts in New York and Washington, D.C., and explore that one subject for thirty minutes. Talking heads, complexity, all of the values shunned by most local news broadcasts are permitted here.

immediate concerns. It was often effective television, and a useful service. Was it news?

On the network level, the news had been preserved in much the same form for twenty years. In part, this caution was a product of the enormous pressures on network news: from government, with official regulatory power over broadcasting through the FCC, and with great informal power such as that applied by the Nixon administration; from Congress and the courts; and from the endless interest groups that all apparently saw in television an unfair portrayal of their concerns.

To give one example of only one kind of pressure: in addition to the equal time provision of the Federal Communications Act requiring broadcasters to give candidates for public office equal access to air time, the FCC and the courts have imposed a "fairness doctrine" on broadcasting. If a broadcast expresses a viewpoint on a controversial issue, its network or station must present all sides of the argument, not necessarily in the same broadcast, but as part of its overall programming. In theory, this was meant to prevent a licensed government monopoly from turning into a propaganda device. In fact, since few broadcasters want to open up their airwaves to unprofitable public affairs debates, the fairness doctrine resulted in the almost total avoidance of controversial issues. Further, any controversial discussion can produce enormous costs. NBC ran up a six-figure bill defending itself from fairness doctrine proceedings concerning a documentary on pensions. And CBS narrowly avoided a congressional contempt citation for failing to turn over notes and tapes from its 1971 documentary *The Selling of the Pentagon.*

Network caution also arose from strong internal pressure; the people who run the network news operations are fully aware of their power. As one NBC news editor put it, "You have no *idea* how seriously the people here take the news." The "happy talk" specter produced by the success of some local news operations cast a shadow over the networks; no one wanted to take part in making the news informal at the network level. This did not mean, however, that the networks were not contemplating whether they, too, had to begin changing and expanding the definition of news. When Barbara Walters, an interviewer on *Today,* was hired away by ABC to coanchor the evening news, the network's executives intended that move as part of a more general reshaping of the evening news.

"The news viewer," said an executive producer, "is drowning in 'news-speak.' He hears more, and understands less, than ever before." ABC wanted to use a longer network news show—forty-five minutes or an hour—to produce features relating to the viewers' personal concerns: raising children, coping with inflation,

Election Day has meant television vigils since the late 1940s. In 1946, the announcer was surrounded by billboard photographs of the candidates. By 1964, Walter Cronkite *(right)* was supported by a more television-conscious studio, as well as the controversial use of computers to predict winners through the use of sample precincts before the total vote was in—and, in some cases, before the polls were closed. The "star" of the 1976 presidential election was NBC's national board *(below)*, which told the viewer who had carried which states.

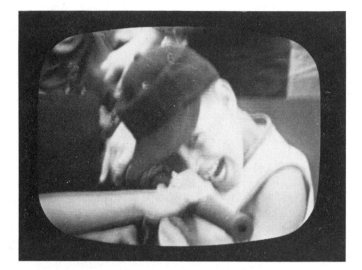

This scene from the controversial CBS documentary "The Selling of the Pentagon" (1971) showed a youngster playing with guns supplied by the Pentagon for public-relations appearances at shopping centers and elsewhere. Charges of distortion led to congressional subpoenas for CBS notes and film; the network refused, and Congress refused to cite the network for contempt.

surviving a divorce. "News," an ABC executive said, "is not just prescheduled government actions and acts of God. It's what's happening out there, to the man or woman watching the show."

ABC's affiliates strongly opposed a longer news show, however, and the network has retreated to a conventional news format. In the process, it learned that more people were interested in what Harry Reasoner and Barbara Walters thought of each other than in what kind of news show ABC was producing. And, in the spring of 1977, ABC put its sports chief, Roone Arledge, in charge of news as well, a remarkable recognition that modern coverage of news and sports are linked together.

There are other signs that network news is indeed changing, although not on the nightly news shows themselves. In 1968, CBS created a prime-time news magazine show, *60 Minutes*, which won high ratings (in part because it was cleverly programmed against two children's shows). That same network later developed a

Barbara Walters, while cohost of *Today,* interviews Henry Kissinger. Her 1976 move to ABC—for a reported salary of a million dollars a year—stirred controversy over mixing news and "personality" on network TV newscasts.

Computer animation is used to add visual impact to public affairs programming, as in this graphic for *The Reasoner Report* on ABC.

A long-running public affairs show, *Today*'s cast in 1976 included critic Gene Shalit, host Tom Brokaw, and feature reporter Betty Furness.

The stars of *60 Minutes*—from left, newsmen Morley Safer, Dan Rather, and Mike Wallace—share a laugh with the program's executive producer, Don Hewitt, right.

Live television coverage can still produce memorable images. This photo shows part of the "Operation Sail" pageantry in New York City during the 1976 bicentennial celebration, the highlight of all-day coverage provided by NBC and CBS during the July Fourth festivities.

In an attempt to move away from the New York–Washington, D.C., news monopoly, Charles Kuralt and his CBS "On the Road" crew have been traveling around the country for more than a decade, finding the small, human-interest shows that leaven the network news.

more gossip-oriented prime-time news show, which failed to achieve the ratings success of *60 Minutes*. Both NBC and ABC are in active pursuit of the thriving gossip trade with shows loosely or directly patterned after *People* magazine, which contains interviews with a varied assortment of celebrities and notables.

As with sports, news on television had become a victim of Heisenberg's uncertainty principle of quantum mechanics—in effect, the act of observation changes the object being observed—which seems to be inevitable with an instrument as powerful as television. It was born to observe, but it could not merely observe. Its presence, its technical possibilities, above all its unparalleled capacity to move in "up close and personal" seemed to change whatever it observed. In the process, it also changed the substance of reality. Television was too powerful to bring reality to its viewers; reality was altered in the process beyond recognition.